# India's Strategic Logic

*Choice Preservation in a Transactional World*

Published by The Constant Variable Project

This work is published by The Constant Variable Project.

Website: longviewpapers.org

Editorial correspondence: contact@longviewpapers.org


ISBNs

979-8-9949638-0-7 : Paperback Edition

979-8-9949638-1-4 : Hardcover Edition

979-8-9949638-2-1 : PDF Edition

**Table of Contents**

# Preface

This book is not a work of advocacy, nor is it a comprehensive history. It is an exercise in orientation. Its purpose is to help the reader—whether citizen, student, or professional—navigate a global environment that has become increasingly fragmented and transactional.

For many observers, India's global behavior in the mid-2020s is read as contradictory. It is often interpreted through inherited frameworks and binary narratives that compress complex strategic choices into categories of "alignment" or "evasion." This book argues that such lenses are insufficient. To understand India is not to search for a final declaration of intent, but to recognize a disciplined method for preserving choice across extended time horizons.

The inquiry unfolds in two parts. The first examines the logic of Indian statecraft: its civilizational anchors, its emergence as a rule-proposer in digital and diplomatic domains, and its refusal to outsource judgment to external systems. The second confronts material reality—the hardcoded frictions of land, resources, and sea that impose gravity on every national ambition.

Understanding these choices does not require agreement. It requires a shift in posture—from consuming events as headlines to interpreting them as structural patterns. This is not a book about what India *is*, but a manual for understanding *why India acts as it does*.

In a world preoccupied with immediacy, the goal here is steadiness of judgment. By focusing on trajectories rather than moments, the book seeks to illuminate the long view

that lends coherence to India's presence in a noisy and uncertain age.


S. Vidhyadharan

# Author's Note

This document examines strategic logic under material constraint. To preserve analytical clarity, it operates within the following guardrails:

Scope and Intent

It is a manual for interpretation, intended to provide functional orientation for citizens, students, and professionals navigating an era of global friction.

The 2026 Baseline

The analysis is anchored in the structural conditions of 2026. While the rapid turnover of geopolitical events is acknowledged, emphasis is placed on factors that evolve more slowly than the news cycle—land, resources, institutional architectures, and infrastructural commitments.

Terminology

Two technical terms form the conceptual spine of this work. Choice Preservation refers to the state's objective of maintaining room for maneuver across multiple global systems without irreversible alignment. Modular Statecraft describes a method of proposing open, non-hierarchical templates for cooperation that others may adopt without surrendering sovereignty.

Data and Interpretation

Priority is given to structural signals—investments, technical standards, institutional mandates, and physical infrastructure—over declarative statements found in speeches, communiqués, or social media. The logic presented here is derived from accumulated patterns of institutional behavior rather than isolated events. Where specific data points are referenced, they are drawn from primary technical records and official baselines available as of 2026.

S. Vidhyadharan

# Acknowledgements

This work did not emerge in isolation. Its arguments reflect years of reading, observation, and conversation—often indirect, sometimes unrecorded—with thinkers, practitioners, and writers whose efforts to understand a changing world have shaped the terrain within which this analysis operates, even where their conclusions differ from those offered here.

Like most attempts at synthesis, it rests on foundations laid by others. Any clarity it achieves owes much to that accumulated work; any errors or misjudgments remain entirely my own.

No institution, organization, or government commissioned, reviewed, or endorsed this manuscript. Its analysis is derived from the observation of accumulated behavior and structural signals. Responsibility for its interpretations, emphases, and omissions rests solely with the author.

S. Vidhyadharan

# Part I: Strategic Logic

# Chapter 1: The Transactional Threshold

The international system that emerged after 1945 no longer functions as a rules-based order in the classical sense. It has transitioned into a transactional environment in which alignment is conditional, commitments are reversible, and access to infrastructure increasingly determines power. This shift is not temporary, nor is it confined to moments of crisis. It represents a new operating condition of global affairs. This chapter examines the threshold—the moment where relationships quietly become transactions.

In this environment, states are evaluated less by their declared positions and more by what they enable, obstruct, or quietly build. Supply chains, standards, energy corridors, data systems, and logistics networks have become instruments of leverage. Cooperation persists, but it is increasingly modular. Alignment is no longer assumed to be durable, and neutrality is not cost-free.

India now operates fully within this transactional threshold.

It is not an emerging observer any longer, adjusting to a system designed by others. Nor is it an external challenger seeking to overturn that system. It is an established participant whose scale, capacity, and relevance place it inside the machinery of global decision-making—even when its behavior resists easy categorization.

This is where misreading begins.

## 1.1 The Interpretive Gap

For many citizens, students, and professionals, India's external behavior appears inconsistent. Headlines report

India's participation in groupings with divergent orientations. A single week may feature engagement with Western technology frameworks alongside energy arrangements with Eurasian suppliers, or development initiatives framed in Global South language alongside security cooperation with advanced economies.

These actions are often forced into binary interpretations: alignment versus autonomy, cooperation versus resistance, values versus interests. When those frames fail, the result is confusion—usually on the part of the observer, not India.

The problem is not a lack of information. It is the persistence of interpretive frameworks that assume the international system still rewards doctrinal alignment and long-term ideological consistency. Those assumptions no longer hold.

India's behavior is not erratic. It is responsive to a system that has itself become transactional, fragmented, and conditional.

## 1.2 Strategic Honesty

A defining feature of India's current posture is strategic honesty—not in rhetoric, but in method. India does not present itself as a guarantor of global order, nor does it claim exemption from the frictions of power. It recognizes that leverage now flows through material capacity, institutional presence, and optionality rather than through declared allegiance.

This recognition produces a style of engagement that is frequently misread as hesitation. In reality, it reflects an unwillingness to over-commit in an environment where commitments are routinely weaponized.

India's objective is not dominance, nor is it detachment. It is the preservation of decision space.

Throughout this book, the term strategic is used in a specific sense. It does not refer to ambition, scale, or intent. It refers to the capacity to preserve choice under constraint—to retain the ability to act tomorrow without being forced by decisions made today.

Within a transactional system, this form of strategic capacity becomes more valuable than declarative certainty.

## 1.3 From Emerging to Established

Much contemporary commentary continues to describe India through the language of emergence. This framing misrepresents India as peripheral, when it is already structurally embedded in global systems. Its economy ranks among the largest in the world. Its digital infrastructure operates at national scale. Its diplomatic and institutional footprint extends across nearly every major multilateral forum.

What has changed is not India's aspiration, but its position. Others increasingly transact with India not as a beneficiary of order, but as a participant whose cooperation affects outcomes.

This shift alters expectations. India is now expected to choose sides, endorse frameworks, and absorb costs in ways previously reserved for established powers. When it resists these expectations, the resistance is often mischaracterized as evasiveness rather than judgment. What appears as ambiguity is often deliberate calibration—an effort to retain room for judgment in systems that demand alignment without offering insulation.

The transactional threshold exposes this tension. India is operating in a system that demands clarity while penalizing over-commitment.

## 1.4 Strategic Choice in a Transactional World

In a transactional environment, alignment is no longer a stable state. It is an ongoing negotiation. Infrastructure replaces ideology as the substrate of influence. Access replaces allegiance as the currency of cooperation.

India's response to this condition is not to reject engagement, but to structure it differently. It favors arrangements that are conditional, modular, and reversible. Reversible, as used here, does not imply hesitation. It refers to choices structured to preserve future flexibility rather than create permanent strategic lock-in. It seeks participation without foreclosure.

India's behavior reflects adaptation to systems whose underlying assumptions do not originate from its own historical trajectory. India's approach is frequently mistaken for ambivalence. It is, instead, a recognition that durability in a fragmented system requires flexibility rather than rigidity.

The chapters that follow examine how this logic operates across domains—digital systems, institutions, infrastructure, energy, land, and maritime space. Before those choices reach negotiating tables or public declarations, they are shaped by constraints that are not political at all.

They are physical.

India's strategic behavior cannot be understood without first examining the frictions imposed by geography, resources, and access. Those constraints form the material reality within which all higher-order decisions are made.

Across the chapters that follow, three structural variables recur: material constraint arising from geographic, resource, and infrastructural realities; preservation of strategic choice; and extended time horizon. Together, they form the framework through which India's external behavior can be interpreted.

# Chapter 2: The Civilizational Operating System

India's strategic behavior cannot be understood through short historical arcs or regime-based analysis alone. It is anchored instead in a long memory of survival across radically different political, economic, and external conditions. This memory functions less as identity and more as constraint—a set of embedded assumptions about continuity, adaptation, and risk.

In practical terms, India behaves as a system that has outlasted repeated shocks. This endurance has produced a preference for strategies that absorb disruption rather than resolve it decisively, and for choices that preserve reversibility rather than enforce finality.

This is not abstraction. It is operational logic.

## 2.1 Continuity Over Rupture

Most modern states are built around rupture: revolutions, wars of independence, ideological resets. Their institutional legitimacy is often tied to a founding moment that marks a sharp break from what came before. As a result, political change is frequently framed as replacement—old systems dismantled, new ones installed.

India's experience is different. Its political forms have changed repeatedly, but its civilizational substrate has persisted. Empires rose and fell, legal systems shifted, administrative languages changed, and external rulers came and went. Yet social organization, economic practices, and cultural continuity adapted rather than collapsed.

This history produces a strategic bias. India tends to treat change as accretive rather than substitutive. New layers are added without fully erasing the old. Systems evolve through absorption, not replacement.

In contemporary policy, this manifests as resistance to irreversible commitments. Decisions are evaluated not only for their immediate payoff, but for their capacity to be unwound if conditions change.

## 2.2 Restoration as a Strategic Threshold

One consequence of this continuity is a distinctive threshold for rupture, the point at which accommodation can no longer be sustained. India does not treat all shocks as existential. It absorbs pressure—economic, diplomatic, or political—longer than many observers expect. This endurance is often mistaken for indecision.

Rupture is reserved for moments where the underlying continuity itself is threatened.

This logic is visible in India's nuclear posture. The decision to cross the nuclear threshold was not framed as transformation, but as restoration—reasserting a strategic equilibrium after repeated external pressures altered the balance. Once that equilibrium was restored, restraint resumed.

The same pattern appears in other domains. India tolerates asymmetry until continuity is at risk. Then it acts decisively, but narrowly. Afterward, it returns to absorption.

This rhythm—endure, restore, stabilize—is a recurring feature of its strategic behavior.

## 2.3 Civilizational Digestion

India's ability to persist has depended on a process that can be described as civilizational digestion. External systems are not rejected outright, nor are they adopted wholesale. They are absorbed, stripped of their conversionary power, and repurposed for domestic stability.

The English legal system provides a clear example. Introduced as a colonial instrument, it was not dismantled after independence. Instead, it was retained, localized, and made compatible with indigenous norms. Its authority was preserved; its ideological orientation was neutralized.

Administrative structures, parliamentary procedures, and even modern economic forms followed a similar path. Tools were kept. Control was internalized.

This pattern continues in contemporary domains—digital infrastructure, regulatory frameworks, and institutional design. India adopts global tools, but resists architectures that require permanent alignment or ideological conformity.

Digestion allows engagement without surrender.

## 2.4 Time as a Strategic Asset

A system that has survived repeated regime changes develops a different relationship with time. Short-term volatility is tolerated if long-term continuity remains intact. This allows India to absorb diplomatic slights, market fluctuations, or temporary isolation without overreacting.

Time becomes a strategic asset rather than a constraint.

This does not imply passivity. Endurance requires institutional memory, administrative capacity, and social cohesion. It also imposes costs. Prolonged ambiguity can frustrate partners, delay benefits, and invite misinterpretation.

India accepts these costs because it values survivability over optimization. A system designed to endure is rarely the most efficient at any single moment, but it is less likely to fracture under stress.

## 2.5 Limits and Trade-offs

This operating system is not without drawbacks. Absorption can slow decision-making. Reversibility can be mistaken for lack of commitment. Long horizons can obscure accountability in the short term.

More importantly, what works for a civilization with deep continuity may not translate to states with different historical trajectories. This is not a template to be exported. It is a constraint to be understood.

India's approach reflects its own accumulated experience. It is shaped by what it has survived, not by what it seeks to impose.

## 2.6 From Culture to Constraint

At this point, the argument must remain grounded. Civilization here is not invoked as identity or pride. It functions as inherited operating logic—a set of defaults that shape how risk, time, and disruption are managed.

These defaults influence how India engages with institutions, technology, and power. They explain why India favors continuity over rupture, restoration over replacement, and absorption over alignment.

They also explain why material constraints matter so deeply.

Civilizational endurance is sustained by access to energy, resources, and supply routes. Without those foundations, absorption fails and continuity fractures.

The next chapter examines how India translates this operating logic into a contemporary method of engagement that allows influence without hierarchy and participation without foreclosure.

That method is modular.

# Chapter 3: Modular Statecraft — The Rule-Proposer Method

India's strategic influence today does not derive primarily from enforcement power or ideological leadership. It emerges from a quieter method: proposing modular systems that others can adopt without surrendering sovereignty or alignment choice.

This chapter defines that method.

India is no longer a passive recipient of inherited global rules, nor does it seek to impose binding architectures on others. Instead, it operates as a rule-proposer—an actor that designs interoperable templates which can be used, adapted, or ignored without penalty.

This is statecraft as architecture.

## 3.1 From Rule-Taker to Rule-Proposer

For much of the post-war period, India operated within frameworks designed elsewhere. Trade rules, financial systems, technological standards, and governance norms were largely inherited. India adapted to them pragmatically, but had limited influence over their design.

As its economic scale and technical capacity grew, this posture became insufficient. India was no longer marginal to the system, yet still constrained by rules it had not shaped.

The conventional response to this transition is to seek rule-making power—control over institutions, veto rights, or enforcement mechanisms. India has largely declined this path.

Instead, it has pursued rule-proposal: offering functional systems that others can opt into without coercion, hierarchy, or exclusivity.

The distinction matters.

A rule-maker enforces compliance.

A rule-taker adapts or resists.

A rule-proposer expands the menu.

## 3.2 Statecraft as Architecture

Modular statecraft treats governance systems the way engineers treat infrastructure: as components that must function across diverse environments.

A modular system has three defining characteristics:

• It performs a narrow, well-defined function.

• It interoperates with other systems without requiring total integration.

• It does not demand ideological or political alignment as a condition of use.

This approach allows adoption without dependency.

India's digital public infrastructure illustrates this logic, but it does not define it. The deeper method lies in how systems are designed: open standards, layered architecture, and voluntary participation.

Countries can use what works, ignore what does not, and retain full control over their internal choices.

Influence is generated not through obligation, but through usefulness.

## 3.3 Choice Without Doctrine

Traditional strategic blocs rely on doctrine—shared values, binding commitments, and aligned narratives. Doctrine simplifies coordination but reduces flexibility. Once adopted, exit becomes costly.

India's method avoids doctrine by design.

By proposing systems rather than alliances, India allows cooperation to remain situational. A country can adopt an Indian-designed payment interface while disagreeing with India on trade. It can participate in a technical standard without aligning politically.

This preserves choice on both sides.

India does not demand exclusivity, and therefore does not incur the cost of enforcement. Others are free to leave without penalty, which paradoxically increases durability.

Systems that do not trap participants are less likely to provoke resistance.

## 3.4 Open Systems, Asymmetric Influence

Modular systems produce a specific form of influence: asymmetric and cumulative.

India does not control how others use these systems, but it shapes the environment in which choices are made. Over time, repeated adoption creates familiarity, lowers transaction costs, and embeds Indian-designed norms into everyday operations.

This is influence without hierarchy.

The effect compounds quietly. No single adoption is decisive. Together, they shift the default architecture of cooperation.

Importantly, this influence is reversible. India accepts that others may modify or replace its proposals. The objective is not permanence, but participation.

## 3.5 Limits and Costs of the Method

Modular statecraft is slower than directive power. It does not generate headlines or immediate leverage. It requires patience, technical competence, and institutional follow-through.

It also risks invisibility. Systems that work quietly are often unnoticed until they fail. Success can be misread as absence.

There is also no guarantee of adoption. Proposals can be ignored. Competing architectures may prevail.

India accepts these risks because the alternative—binding others through doctrine or enforcement—would undermine its own preference for autonomy and reversibility.

This method reflects India's operating logic, not an aspiration to leadership in the conventional sense.

## 3.6 From Architecture to Material Reality

Rules and systems do not operate in abstraction. They are tested against physical constraints—geography, energy flows, supply routes, and security of access.

A digital standard matters only if cables carry data.

A payment system functions only if energy grids remain stable.

A governance template endures only if material flows are uninterrupted.

This is where modular statecraft meets reality.

The chapters that follow shift from method to constraint. Before choices are debated in institutions or proposed through systems, they are shaped by land, resources, and sea.

The logic remains the same: preserve choice, avoid foreclosure, and build resilience against uncertainty.

But the terrain hardens.


*The logic introduced in these chapters explains how India thinks; the chapters that follow explain what this logic must contend with. While rules can be proposed in digital or diplomatic space, they are ultimately tested against the hard realities of maritime chokepoints and the friction of the landmass. Statecraft, no matter how patient or carefully structured, remains anchored to the gravity of geography. We move now from the architecture of choice to the constraints of the land itself.*

# Chapter 4: Multi-Alignment as Active Design: Engagement Without Camps

This chapter examines alignment not as affiliation, but as design. It argues that India's multi-alignment is not an avoidance of choice, but an active method of engagement in systems that reward commitment to camps.

## 4.1 From Non-Alignment to Multi-Alignment

For much of the twentieth century, India's foreign policy was shaped by a logic of abstention. Classical non-alignment emerged in a bipolar world where power was concentrated, choices were narrow, and misalignment carried existential risk. The objective was not influence but survival. Staying out of great-power rivalry was a way to avoid being absorbed, coerced, or crushed by forces far larger than the newly independent state.

Non-alignment, in this context, was a strategy of absence. It sought distance from competing blocs, limited participation in their security architectures, and emphasized moral positioning over institutional embedding. Presence in global forums existed, but it was selective and often symbolic. The primary aim was to avoid entanglement rather than to shape outcomes.

That logic no longer describes India's position in the world.

By 2026, the international system has moved beyond rigid bipolarity, and India has moved beyond marginal leverage. Global power is distributed across multiple centers. Rules are written not only through treaties, but through standards bodies, financial institutions, supply chains, and technological architectures. In this environment, absence does not preserve autonomy. It forfeits it. This shift has been reinforced by a global environment in which major powers increasingly treat engagement as transactional, making absence from decision-making forums a greater risk than participation.

Multi-alignment represents a fundamental shift from abstention to presence.

Rather than standing apart, India now seeks to be present wherever consequential decisions are being shaped. This presence is not about allegiance. It is about agency. India's objective is not to choose camps, but to ensure that no durable global rule is written without its participation, input, or capacity to influence design.

This explains why India simultaneously occupies spaces that earlier frameworks would have treated as mutually exclusive. It participates as an observer in G7 processes while chairing BRICS+. It engages deeply with the Quad while maintaining strategic partnerships across Eurasia, the Middle East, and the Global South. It works within established Western-led institutions while supporting the creation of parallel mechanisms where existing ones fail to reflect contemporary realities.

This ubiquity is often mischaracterized as indecision or opportunism. In fact, it reflects a sober reassessment of where influence now resides. In a fragmented system, influence accrues not from loyalty to a bloc, but from sustained presence across forums that address different dimensions of national interest.

Multi-alignment thus replaces neutrality with sovereign agency. Neutrality implied standing between others. Sovereign agency implies standing everywhere that matters.

The distinction is crucial. Neutrality was reactive. It responded to external pressures by avoiding choice. Multi-alignment is proactive. It creates choices by embedding India into multiple systems simultaneously. Where nonalignment reduced exposure by minimizing contact, multi-alignment manages exposure by diversifying it.

This shift also reflects India's growing internal capacity. Sustained presence across multiple platforms requires diplomatic depth, economic scale, and institutional endurance. India would not pursue this strategy if it lacked the ability to absorb complexity over time. Multi-alignment is therefore not aspirational. It is operational, grounded in an assessment of what India can now sustain.

Most importantly, presence changes the nature of influence. India does not need to dominate a forum to shape its trajectory. Regular participation, procedural engagement, and early involvement in agenda-setting allow India to nudge outcomes long before positions harden. Influence is exercised upstream, not through last-minute declarations.

In this sense, multi-alignment is less about signaling intent and more about shaping environments. It ensures that India is present when assumptions are formed, standards are drafted, and defaults are chosen. Once these are set, alignment choices narrow rapidly. Presence keeps them open.

This transition from abstention to presence marks a decisive break with the past. India is no longer protecting autonomy by staying out. It is protecting autonomy by being everywhere that matters—on its own terms, without exclusivity, and without surrendering the right to differ.

## 4.2 Engagement Without Camps

Multi-alignment operates on the premise that global challenges are not neatly partitioned into ideological camps. Security, trade, technology, climate, and development intersect in ways that resist binary classification. India's approach accepts this complexity rather than attempting to simplify it.

Participation in security dialogues, development institutions, and regional groupings is therefore not treated as mutually exclusive. India engages where interests overlap and disengages where they do not. This selective participation is often mistaken for hedging. In practice, it reflects a refusal to subordinate all interests to a single organizing principle.

By avoiding permanent camps, India preserves autonomy of judgment. It retains the ability to cooperate on one issue while disagreeing on another. This flexibility is not cost-free. It requires sustained diplomatic effort and tolerance for external criticism. But it also prevents the foreclosure of future options.

## 4.3 The Quad and BRICS+: Parallel Engagements and Simultaneous Diplomacy

India's simultaneous engagement with the Quad and BRICS+ is often treated as the clearest illustration of its multi-aligned posture—and the most frequently misunderstood. External commentary tends to frame these engagements as acts of balancing, as though India were weighing one grouping against the other to extract advantage or hedge against uncertainty. This interpretation imposes a zero-sum logic on arrangements that were never designed to operate in opposition.

From India's perspective, the Quad and BRICS+ serve fundamentally different national functions. They are not competing affiliations, but parallel instruments addressing distinct layers of the international system.

The Quad operates primarily in the security and high-technology domains. Its core concerns include maritime stability, freedom of navigation, supply chain resilience, and coordination among technologically advanced democracies. For India, participation in the Quad strengthens its ability to secure the maritime commons that underpin its trade flows, energy imports, and regional connectivity. It also provides a platform for cooperation on emerging technologies where trust, interoperability, and standards alignment matter.

BRICS+, by contrast, is oriented toward the economic architecture of the Global South. Its focus lies in development finance, institutional reform, and the redistribution of voice within global economic governance. These challenges do not arise from hostile actors, but from the internal mechanics of global development systems that shape access to capital and policy autonomy. Through BRICS+, India engages with countries facing similar constraints in access to capital, infrastructure financing, and policy space. The forum functions as a vehicle for addressing systemic asymmetries rather than immediate security threats.

Seen this way, the two engagements are complementary rather than contradictory. The Quad secures the external environment in which India's trade and technology flows operate. BRICS+ addresses the internal mechanics of development and financial inclusion that shape long-term growth trajectories. One manages risk; the other expands capacity. These engagements rarely advance in parallel or with equal intensity, yet India treats such asymmetry as normal rather than as a signal to rebalance.

India's 2026 BRICS+ chairmanship illustrates this division of labor clearly. Rather than pushing the grouping toward ideological opposition or symbolic rupture—such as calls for forced de-dollarization or the creation of a rival monetary bloc—India has steered discussions toward practical reforms. These include strengthening development financing mechanisms, improving access to climate capital, and increasing the responsiveness of multilateral institutions to emerging-economy needs.

At the same time, India's engagement with the Quad has deepened through operational cooperation in maritime domain awareness, disaster response, and supply chain coordination. These initiatives are not rhetorical. They address immediate vulnerabilities in shipping lanes, critical infrastructure, and technology ecosystems that directly affect India's security and economic stability.

What enables this simultaneous diplomacy is India's refusal to collapse all external relationships into a single strategic narrative. Engagements are compartmentalized by function, not subordinated to a master alignment. Participation in one forum does not require signaling against another. Disagreement in one domain does not invalidate cooperation in others.

This functional separation is deliberate. It allows India to absorb pressure without cascading commitment. When tensions rise in one arena, they do not automatically force realignment across the board. This reduces escalation risk and preserves room for maneuver.

Importantly, India does not treat either forum as a substitute for the other. The Quad does not replace engagement with emerging economies, nor does BRICS+ substitute for cooperation with advanced democracies. Each fills gaps the other cannot. Reliance on only one would create strategic blind spots.

Critics often ask whether this posture can be sustained as global competition intensifies. India's answer, implicit in its actions, is that sustainability lies precisely in avoiding exclusivity. Alignment simplifies choices in the short term but concentrates risk over time. Parallel engagement distributes that risk across systems with different incentives, cycles, and fault lines.

Simultaneous diplomacy therefore reflects a design choice rather than a temporary accommodation. It allows India to influence multiple conversations at once, to moderate extremes within each, and to retain autonomy across shifting geopolitical landscapes. The Quad and BRICS+ are not weights on opposite ends of a scale. They are tools in different hands, used for different tasks, in pursuit of the same underlying objective: preserving strategic choice in a fragmented world.

## 4.4 The Digital and Technological Dimension of Multi-Alignment: Avoiding Digital Enclosure

Multi-alignment in 2026 is no longer confined to diplomacy and security. Increasingly, it is shaped by decisions made in laboratories, data centers, standards bodies, and software architectures. Technology has become one of the primary mechanisms through which alignment is enforced, often implicitly. Choices about digital infrastructure, data governance, and artificial intelligence can lock countries into ecosystems that are difficult to exit, creating forms of dependence that are more durable than formal alliances.

India's approach to this challenge reflects a clear strategic concern: avoiding digital enclosure.

Digital enclosure occurs when a country's core systems—communications, identity, payments, data, or computation—become tightly coupled to a single external provider or governance model. Once embedded, these systems constrain policy autonomy, limit bargaining power, and narrow future choices. Alignment is no longer a matter of diplomatic preference; it is embedded in code[1].

India has sought to resist this outcome not by rejecting external partnerships, but by designing bridges between systems rather than adopting any single one wholesale. This logic underpins India's engagement with advanced technology partners while simultaneously proposing open, modular frameworks for broader adoption.

A clear example is India's participation in the U.S.–India Initiative on Critical and Emerging Technology (iCET). Through this mechanism, India collaborates closely with the United States on semiconductors, quantum technologies, artificial intelligence, and defense-related innovation. These engagements are deep, technical, and consequential. They reflect recognition that access to frontier research and high-end manufacturing ecosystems is essential for India's technological advancement.

At the same time, India has resisted adopting "black box" systems that would subordinate its digital future to any single external architecture. Instead of importing closed platforms, India has emphasized open standards, interoperability, and domestic capacity building. The objective is not technological self-sufficiency in isolation, but technological sovereignty through optionality.

This dual approach is visible in India's promotion of Digital Public Infrastructure (DPI) as a global template. By offering DPI components—identity, payments, document storage, and data exchange—as open-source, interoperable modules, India proposes an alternative pathway for digital modernization. Countries adopting these systems are not required to align with a particular geopolitical camp. They

---

[1] In this book, "code" refers to software code and digital system logic, not legal or statutory codes.

can integrate with multiple providers, customize governance arrangements, and retain control over data flows.

The same logic is now being extended to artificial intelligence. Rather than asserting regulatory authority, India has focused on shaping access and architectural choices in emerging technology ecosystems. This approach is visible in India's efforts to bring together governments, researchers, and firms around questions of AI access, safety, and capacity-building, including through initiatives such as the India AI Impact Summit. Instead of framing AI governance as a contest between regulation and innovation, India has emphasized infrastructure—access to compute, shared datasets, and public-interest models that lower entry barriers for researchers and startups in the Global South.

This infrastructure-first approach reflects a broader strategic insight. Control over standards and interfaces often matters more than control over applications. By influencing how systems connect, India shapes the environment in which technological choices are made without dictating outcomes.

Avoiding digital enclosure also shapes India's position on data governance. India treats data neither as an unrestricted corporate asset nor as a centralized state resource. Instead, it emphasizes consent-based frameworks and layered access. This position does not align neatly with existing models, and India has resisted pressure to conform to any single template. The goal is not to define a universal doctrine of data governance, but to preserve the ability to adapt as technologies and risks evolve.

Multi-alignment in the digital domain therefore operates through architecture rather than alignment. India collaborates deeply with technologically advanced partners while ensuring that its core systems remain interoperable, modular, and open to multiple futures. It builds bridges between ecosystems rather than walls around them.

This approach carries costs. Open systems are harder to secure and govern than closed ones. Interoperability demands sustained coordination and institutional capacity. But the alternative—digital enclosure—carries far greater long-term risks. Once locked into a single technological regime, strategic autonomy erodes silently, beyond the reach of diplomatic correction.

By treating digital and technological choices as matters of geopolitical design rather than procurement, India extends its multi-aligned strategy into the most consequential domain of the coming decades. The objective remains consistent with earlier chapters: preserving choice, distributing risk, and ensuring that engagement expands options rather than forecloses them.

## 4.5 Managing the Middle-Income Trap as a Geopolitical Goal

For India, multi-alignment is not only a foreign policy posture. It is also an economic strategy shaped by a narrow and time-bound growth window. The risk of middle-income stagnation—where growth slows before a country achieves broad-based prosperity—has become one of the most consequential constraints on India's long-term autonomy. Avoiding this outcome has increasingly begun to shape aspects of India's geopolitical thinking.

The so-called middle-income trap is less a fixed rule than a pattern many developing economies seem to encounter. As wages rise, the low-cost labor advantage that initially drew investment gradually fades, shifting the basis of competitiveness toward productivity, skills, infrastructure, and technological capability. If those upgrades don't keep pace, growth can slow even while public expectations continue to rise. The result is a more demanding economic environment: policy choices narrow, inequality pressures become more visible, and external vulnerabilities can increase just as domestic ambitions are expanding.

India's response to this risk has been to keep its external economic environment as open and diversified as possible. Trade diversification across advanced and emerging economies is treated not as diplomacy for its own sake, but as insulation against growth stagnation and external shocks. Multi-alignment serves this purpose by preventing over-dependence on any single source of capital, technology, energy, or market access. It allows India to draw simultaneously from multiple growth channels, each contributing different inputs to its development trajectory.

Engagement with advanced economies provides access to high-end capital, frontier technologies, and managerial expertise. These inputs are essential for moving up global value chains, particularly in manufacturing, semiconductors, pharmaceuticals, and digital services. At the same time, sustained engagement with the Global South ensures access to energy resources, raw materials, and expanding consumer markets that support scale and resilience.

This dual engagement is not opportunistic. It reflects an understanding that no single bloc can supply all the conditions required for sustained growth. Over-alignment with capital-rich economies risks technological dependence and trade imbalances. Over-reliance on resource-exporting partners risks stagnation and limited productivity gains. Multi-alignment keeps both pathways open.

Trade diversification is a central element of this strategy. India has resisted the temptation to lock itself into narrow trade architectures that prioritize efficiency over resilience. Instead, it has pursued a mix of bilateral agreements, regional partnerships, and selective protection where domestic capacity-building is at stake. The objective is not maximal integration, but strategic integration aligned with long-term growth.

Energy security further illustrates this logic. India's growth trajectory requires reliable and affordable energy at scale. Multi-alignment allows India to source energy across regions and regimes, reducing exposure to geopolitical shocks. Simultaneously, participation in climate finance initiatives and renewable energy alliances supports the transition toward a more sustainable energy mix without sacrificing development momentum.

The same reasoning applies to infrastructure and manufacturing. By engaging with multiple partners across financing, construction, and technology transfer, India avoids becoming captive to any single model or supplier. This flexibility is particularly important as global supply chains reconfigure in response to geopolitical fragmentation.

Managing the middle-income risk also shapes India's diplomatic restraint. Rapid growth requires predictability. Excessive confrontation, symbolic alignment, or ideological posturing introduces volatility that can deter investment and disrupt trade. Multi-alignment provides a stabilizing framework within which India can pursue reform, absorb shocks, and maintain growth continuity.

Seen in this light, multi-alignment is less about global positioning and more about domestic survival at scale. It is a tool for preserving economic momentum during a critical transition phase. The ultimate measure of success is not diplomatic applause, but sustained improvement in productivity, employment, and institutional capacity.

By linking foreign policy choices to the hard constraint of economic transformation, India grounds its multi-aligned strategy in necessity rather than ambition. Growth is not a side effect of geopolitics. It is one of its primary drivers.

## 4.6 Costs, Critiques, and Constraints

Multi-alignment, while strategically coherent, is not costless. It imposes a persistent "bandwidth tax" on the state—diplomatic, institutional, and cognitive. Managing parallel engagements across security, economic, techno-logical, and development domains requires sustained attention, interpretive clarity, and administrative depth. The very flexibility that preserves autonomy also increases the burden of coordination.

One risk inherent in this approach is strategic exhaustion. Unlike alliance-based systems, where commitments simplify decision-making by narrowing choices, multi-alignment demands continuous judgment. Positions must be calibrated, signals must be managed, and inconsistencies must be explained. This places pressure on diplomatic institutions and requires a high tolerance for ambiguity—both internally and externally. Tolerance for ambiguity, as used here, does not imply uncertainty of purpose; it reflects a deliberate choice to preserve strategic flexibility in a world where rigid alignment can become a liability.

In 2026, these pressures are amplified by the return of transactional politics in several major capitals. Leaders accustomed to loyalty-based frameworks often view flexibility as unreliability. Requests for alignment are framed as tests of commitment. India's refusal to meet these expectations can generate friction, particularly in moments of crisis when rapid declarations are valued over sustained cooperation.

India's response to this critique has been consistent: reliability matters more than alignment. India may not vote predictably across all issues, but it seeks to be dependable in specific domains—maritime safety, humanitarian assistance, vaccine production, disaster response, and infrastructure delivery. Trust is built through performance rather than pledges.

This distinction is not always well received. Multi-alignment resists the emotional clarity of camp-based politics. It frustrates narratives that divide the world into allies and adversaries. Yet India has judged that the long-term cost of interpretive friction is lower than the structural risk of dependency.

There are also domestic constraints. Sustaining multi-alignment requires institutional continuity across political cycles, bureaucratic coordination across ministries, and public understanding of why apparent inconsistencies serve national interest. Without interpretive clarity, flexibility can be mistaken for drift, and restraint can be misread as hesitation.

This is where the need for clear frameworks becomes evident. Multi-alignment works only if its logic is understood internally as well as externally. Otherwise, the strategy risks being undermined by miscommunication, unrealistic expectations, or reactive policy shifts.

Despite these challenges, India has chosen to bear the bandwidth cost. The alternative—premature alignment within a fragmented global order—would reduce choices precisely when adaptability is most valuable.

## 4.7 Interpreting Multi-Alignment Correctly

Understanding multi-alignment as active design rather than indecision is essential to interpreting India's actions.

The absence of permanent alignment does not indicate lack of strategy. It reflects a deliberate choice to manage complexity rather than deny it.

For the observer, the key is to track consistency over time rather than alignment at a moment. India's positions may vary by issue, but patterns persist: a preference for optionality, resistance to exclusivity, and emphasis on autonomy. Reliability is demonstrated through performance in specific domains, not through uniform voting behavior or declarative loyalty.

Multi-alignment allows India to absorb shocks, manage transitions, and adjust its trajectory without committing to irreversible paths. In doing so, it completes the argument developed in the preceding chapters: India's engagement without camps is the operational expression of its civilizational time horizons and its method of rule-proposing without doctrine. This is not a transitional phase or a tactical pause. It is a durable way of operating in a plural, fragmented world where stability must be managed rather than assumed.

**Chapter Conclusion**

Multi-alignment, as practiced by India, is not a temporary posture adopted in an unsettled world. It is a durable response to systems that demand premature commitment while offering limited insulation from downstream risk. By engaging multiple frameworks without collapsing into any single camp, India preserves the ability to judge, adjust, and recalibrate as conditions change. What appears externally as ambivalence is, internally, a disciplined refusal to confuse participation with surrender.

This form of engagement carries costs. It requires patience, absorbs misinterpretation, and forgoes the short-term clarity that alignment with a dominant bloc can provide. Yet it also retains freedom of action in a world where commitments are increasingly irreversible. Multi-alignment, in this sense, is not a rejection of order but an insistence on participating in it without forfeiting autonomy. It is a strategy shaped less by preference than by design. Multi-alignment, in this sense, is not indecision but a deliberate refusal to exchange long-term autonomy for short-term geopolitical simplicity.

# Chapter 5: Strategic Autonomy as Choice Preservation

This chapter defines strategic autonomy not as distance from the world, but as a governing logic for preserving freedom of judgment within it. It examines how India remains deeply engaged in global systems without allowing any single system to dictate its domestic priorities or external responses. Autonomy is presented not as an end state or ideological stance, but as a continuous practice: managing interdependence in ways that protect decision-making capacity under pressure.

## 5.1 From Independence to Interdependence

In the decades following independence, strategic autonomy was primarily defensive. The international system India entered after 1947 was structured by power asymmetries it could not influence and institutions it did not design. Autonomy, under those conditions, meant minimizing exposure. Staying out of binding alliances, avoiding entangling commitments, and limiting dependence on external systems were rational responses to a world in which coercion was common and leverage flowed overwhelmingly in one direction.

That logic no longer maps cleanly onto the present environment.

By the mid-2020s, India is no longer a peripheral participant navigating systems designed elsewhere. It is a central actor embedded across trade, finance, technology, energy, and security networks. Complete disengagement from these systems is neither possible nor desirable. The challenge has shifted from avoiding influence to managing it.

Strategic autonomy in this context does not mean insulation from interdependence. It means resilience within it.

The defining shift is from autonomy as separation to autonomy as decision-making resilience. India now operates in a world where staying out of global systems would reduce autonomy rather than preserve it. Absence forfeits influence, restricts options, and increases vulnerability to external shocks. The contemporary task is therefore inverted: remain present, but ensure that presence does not become paralysis.

Decision-making resilience refers to the ability to maintain a domestic policy course even when global systems are under stress, fragmented, or weaponized. It is not about eliminating dependence, but about preventing dependence from becoming decisive. A resilient state can absorb external pressure, recalibrate partnerships, and adjust tactics without being forced into binary choices.

This evolution reflects changes both in India's capabilities and in the global environment itself. As India's economic scale, technological capacity, and diplomatic reach have expanded, so too has its exposure. Supply chains, capital flows, data networks, and security arrangements now intersect directly with domestic governance. Autonomy can no longer be preserved by distance. It must be engineered through design.

The move from independence to interdependence therefore does not represent a loss of autonomy. It represents a redefinition of it. Strategic autonomy becomes the capacity to remain embedded without becoming captive, to cooperate without surrendering judgment, and to participate without pre-committing to outcomes dictated elsewhere.

This redefinition sets the foundation for the sections that follow. Alignment, in such a system, is no longer a guarantee of stability. Choice preservation becomes the primary metric by which autonomy is exercised and evaluated.

## 5.2 Autonomy vs. Alignment in a Transactional World

Alignment has traditionally been understood as a stabilizing force. By tying one's interests to a larger power or bloc, a state could reduce uncertainty, gain security assurances, and simplify decision-making. In a loyalty-based international order, alignment functioned as a form of insurance: commitments were durable, expectations were predictable, and deviations were costly for all parties involved.

That environment no longer exists.

The global order of the mid-2020s is increasingly transactional. Partnerships are evaluated through short-term cost–benefit calculations, domestic political cycles exert outsized influence, and commitments are frequently revised or withdrawn. Trade preferences, security assurances, and technological access are no longer treated as enduring arrangements but as conditional instruments. Alignment, under these conditions, carries hidden costs.

The most significant of these costs is exposure to sudden shifts in partner priorities. When relationships are framed transactionally, loyalty is neither assumed nor rewarded. A partner's internal political realignment, economic shock, or strategic recalculation can rapidly alter the terms of engagement. States that have over-invested in a single alignment pathway may find themselves constrained precisely when flexibility is most needed.

Strategic autonomy functions as a response to this volatility. Rather than betting on the permanence of any one partnership, India treats relationships as contingent and revisable. This does not imply distrust or opportunism. It reflects an assessment of how contemporary power operates. In a system where commitments are reversible, resilience comes from maintaining multiple pathways rather than deepening exclusive ones.

This logic is best understood as an insurance mechanism. Just as financial diversification reduces exposure to market shocks, diplomatic and economic diversification reduces exposure to political shocks. If one partner restricts trade, technology transfer, or security cooperation, an autonomous India retains alternative routes. The cost of maintaining these options may be higher in the short term, but the long-term benefit is freedom of action.

Alignment also carries a subtler risk: it narrows the space for independent judgment. When a state is deeply embedded in a single bloc, policy choices increasingly reflect alliance maintenance rather than domestic priorities. Decisions begin to anticipate partner reactions rather than respond to internal needs. Over time, strategic thinking shifts from problem-solving to signaling.

India has sought to avoid this trap by separating cooperation from convergence. It engages deeply where interests align, but resists pressures to universalize those alignments across unrelated domains. A security partnership does not automatically imply economic conformity. A technological collaboration does not require political endorsement. Each engagement is evaluated on its own terms.

This approach often frustrates external observers accustomed to binary commitments. The expectation of alignment simplifies interpretation: friends act predictably, adversaries do not. Strategic autonomy complicates this narrative. It replaces predictability with consistency of method rather than consistency of position.

The transactional nature of the current global order makes this distinction essential. When partners themselves reserve the right to revise commitments, strategic autonomy becomes less a posture of caution and more a requirement for stability. It allows India to participate fully without surrendering the capacity to adjust when conditions change.

Autonomy, in this sense, is not an alternative to engagement. It is a way of engaging without becoming structurally dependent on assumptions of permanence that no longer hold.

## 5.3 Choice Preservation as the Core Metric

Strategic autonomy becomes operational only when it is translated into a usable decision rule. Without such a rule, autonomy risks remaining a rhetorical preference rather than a governing logic. In India's contemporary practice, that rule can be stated simply: major policies should be evaluated by whether they preserve or foreclose future choices.

This principle replaces ideological or declarative tests with a functional one. Instead of asking whether a decision signals alignment, strength, or resolve, the more relevant question becomes whether it expands the range of options available under future uncertainty. Policies that lock the state into rigid dependencies may appear efficient or decisive in the short term, but they reduce adaptability when conditions change. Choice preservation treats flexibility itself as a strategic asset.

This logic is especially relevant in an environment characterized by volatility rather than equilibrium. When external systems are stable and commitments durable, optimizing for efficiency makes sense. When systems are prone to fragmentation, sanctions, or politicization, resilience becomes more valuable than optimization. Strategic autonomy prioritizes the latter.

The choice-preservation test does not demand indecision or delay. It demands discrimination. Some choices are reversible; others are not. Entering a trade arrangement that allows exit or adjustment carries different risks from adopting a closed technological platform that cannot be replaced without systemic disruption. Strategic autonomy seeks to be selective about where irreversibility is accepted and where it is avoided.

This framework also explains decisions that may appear suboptimal when judged narrowly. India may choose a more expensive energy source, a slower technology rollout, or a more complex supply chain not because it lacks alternatives, but because diversification preserves the ability to switch if primary channels become politically conditional. The additional cost functions as an insurance premium against future coercion.

Choice preservation also operates across time horizons. Some policies preserve short-term flexibility at the expense of long-term capacity, while others do the opposite. Strategic autonomy requires balancing these horizons rather than privileging one automatically. Investments in domestic capability, even when inefficient initially, can expand future choices by reducing reliance on external suppliers.

Importantly, this metric does not imply that all options must remain open indefinitely. Strategic autonomy accepts that some commitments are necessary and beneficial. The distinction lies in intent. Commitments are entered with an awareness of their locking effects and with compensating measures elsewhere to prevent systemic dependence.

For the observer, choice preservation offers a clearer lens than alignment or intention. When India declines one proposal while advancing another, the pattern to look for is not inconsistency but option management. Declining an option that preserves flexibility can be more strategic than accepting one that narrows future choices.

By elevating choice preservation as the core metric, strategic autonomy becomes legible as a disciplined practice rather than an evasive posture. It is a way of governing uncertainty by ensuring that today's decisions do not become tomorrow's constraints.

## 5.4 Economic Autonomy Without Economic Closure

Strategic autonomy in the economic domain is often misunderstood as a preference for self-sufficiency. This misunderstanding is understandable. In earlier phases of India's development, self-sufficiency functioned as a domestic slogan shaped by scarcity, limited bargaining power, and external vulnerability.

The contemporary meaning is different. India's current approach does not seek economic closure, nor does it revive earlier inward-focused models of development. Economic autonomy, as practiced today, is not about withdrawing from global markets but about shaping the terms on which integration occurs.

India's economy is deeply interdependent. Growth depends on access to capital, technology, energy, and markets beyond its borders. Any attempt at economic closure would impose costs far greater than the risks it seeks to avoid. Strategic autonomy therefore operates through diversification rather than insulation. The objective is not to minimize exposure, but to prevent exposure from becoming leverage.

Diversification functions as a shield. By engaging across multiple trade corridors, financial systems, and supply chains, India reduces the ability of any single partner to dictate internal economic policy. When trade, investment, or regulatory access is distributed rather than concentrated, external pressure loses effectiveness. Autonomy is preserved not by refusing integration, but by preventing monopolization of influence.

This logic explains India's preference for multiple, overlapping economic arrangements rather than exclusive trade architectures. Bilateral and regional agreements are pursued selectively, with an emphasis on preserving regulatory space and exit options. No single agreement is treated as indispensable. The cumulative effect is an economic network that is dense but not rigid.

Capital flows illustrate this approach clearly. India remains open to global investment and venture capital, particularly in sectors where scale and innovation are essential. At the same time, it maintains control over core digital and financial infrastructure. The objective is to welcome capital without allowing capital to dictate governance frameworks. Ownership of platforms, standards, and data architectures remains a sovereign concern even as markets remain open.

Energy policy further reinforces this pattern. India's growth trajectory requires reliable energy at scale, yet energy dependence has historically been a source of vulnerability. Strategic autonomy therefore emphasizes diversification of sources, routes, and technologies. Fossil fuels, renewables, and emerging energy systems coexist not as transitional compromises, but as parallel pathways that reduce exposure to disruption.

Economic autonomy also involves accepting trade-offs. Diversified supply chains may be less efficient than optimized ones. Domestic capacity-building may raise short-term costs. Maintaining regulatory flexibility may slow negotiations by keeping open the possibility of future regulatory action. These costs are not accidental; they are consciously absorbed as the price of resilience. Strategic autonomy treats resilience as an economic input rather than a residual benefit.

Crucially, this approach does not reject global integration. It reframes it. Integration expands national capability without foreclosing policy choice. The measure of success is not maximal openness or minimal protection, but sustained growth without structural dependency.

For citizens and businesses, this distinction matters. Economic autonomy is not a retreat from globalization, nor a signal of inward turn. It is an attempt to ensure that participation in global markets strengthens domestic capacity rather than substitutes for it.

In this sense, economic autonomy functions as an enabling condition. It supports growth, buffers shocks, and preserves the freedom to adjust course when global conditions shift. Closure narrows choices. Diversification preserves them.

## 5.5 Security Autonomy and Threshold Management

Strategic autonomy in the security domain is often misunderstood as a reluctance to commit or an aversion to partnerships. In practice, it reflects a different organizing principle: threshold management. India's security posture is designed to ensure that no external actor becomes indispensable for managing escalation, deterrence, or crisis response in its immediate environment.

At the core of this approach is the recognition that security guarantees, like economic arrangements, have become increasingly conditional. External assurances may weaken, be reinterpreted, or be withdrawn as priorities shift. Strategic autonomy therefore prioritizes survivability and redundancy over reliance. The objective is not dominance, but the ability to absorb shocks and manage escalation without being forced into choices dictated by others.

Threshold management refers to the capacity to control the level and direction of conflict without crossing points that would require external intervention. India seeks sufficient indigenous capability to respond credibly to regional contingencies, deter escalation, and stabilize situations before they exceed manageable bounds. This does not imply isolation from partners, but it does require that core security decisions remain domestically anchored.

Indigenous capacity plays a central role in this logic. Investments in domestic defense production, command-and-control systems, and strategic deterrence are not expressions of self-reliance for its own sake. They are mechanisms for preserving freedom of judgment during crises. When a state lacks the means to act independently at critical moments, autonomy becomes theoretical rather than practical.

Partnerships are therefore structured as force multipliers rather than substitutes. Military exercises, interoperability initiatives, and technology cooperation are pursued to enhance flexibility, not to integrate command structures or pre-commit responses. India values the ability to work alongside multiple partners while retaining discretion over when, how, and whether to act.

This distinction is subtle but consequential. Interoperability by choice allows collaboration without obligation. Integration by default narrows options and introduces expectations that may not align with domestic assessments during a crisis. Strategic autonomy favors the former because it preserves room for calibrated response.

Security autonomy also shapes India's approach to escalation control. Rather than framing challenges in existential terms, India tends to manage conflict along a spectrum, distinguishing between provocation, pressure, and rupture. This graduated view allows responses to be proportionate and reversible. It reduces the risk that external actors interpret every incident as a trigger for alliance activation.

The emphasis on redundancy further reinforces this posture. Multiple supply lines, diversified partnerships, and layered capabilities reduce the likelihood that a single failure cascades into systemic vulnerability. Redundancy may appear inefficient in peacetime, but it becomes decisive under stress.

For observers, this approach can be misread as caution or ambiguity. In reality, it reflects a disciplined assessment of risk in an environment where security commitments are no longer absolute. Strategic autonomy in security policy is not about standing alone. It is about ensuring that cooperation enhances capability without constraining judgment.

By managing thresholds rather than seeking guarantees, India preserves the ability to respond to evolving threats on its own terms. This capacity to act without compulsion is what gives strategic autonomy its practical meaning in the security domain.

## 5.6 Technology, Standards, and Autonomy

In the contemporary global order, strategic autonomy is increasingly embedded not in treaties or declarations, but in systems. Technology has become one of the primary arenas in which dependence is created and autonomy constrained. Choices about platforms, standards, and architectures can quietly determine the limits of policy long before diplomatic options are exercised.

This shift changes how autonomy must be understood. Control over physical territory or military assets, while still necessary, is no longer sufficient. States that lack influence over digital infrastructure, data flows, and technical standards may find their administrative and economic systems vulnerable to external leverage without any formal breach of sovereignty.

India's response has been to treat technology as an element of statecraft rather than procurement. Strategic autonomy in this domain is pursued through architectural choices that preserve optionality. The emphasis is not on excluding foreign technology, but on avoiding closed systems that cannot be adapted, audited, or replaced.

In this context, "optionality" does not mean avoiding commitments or delaying decisions indefinitely. It refers to preserving the ability to adjust course as conditions change. A policy increases optionality if it keeps multiple future paths open and reduces the cost of switching between them. Conversely, early lock-in—whether technological, contractual, or institutional—may deliver short-term certainty but often narrows long-term choice.

Open standards play a central role in this logic. By favoring interoperable systems over proprietary ones, India reduces the risk that critical public functions can be disrupted by decisions made outside its jurisdiction. Interoperability allows components to be substituted over time, ensuring that technological dependence does not harden into structural constraint.

This approach is visible in India's investment in Digital Public Infrastructure (DPI). Systems for identity, payments, and document exchange are designed as modular layers rather than monolithic platforms. Governance remains domestic, while interfaces remain open. This separation allows India to integrate globally without surrendering administrative control.

Strategic autonomy also shapes India's participation in standards-setting bodies. Rather than adopting frameworks wholesale, India seeks to influence how standards are defined, particularly in areas where early decisions can lock in long-term dependencies. Presence in these forums is treated as a form of risk management. Absence would allow others to shape rules to which India would later have to adapt.

The same logic applies to emerging technologies such as artificial intelligence. Instead of framing autonomy as control over specific models or outcomes, India focuses on access to foundational inputs: compute, data, and talent. Control over outcomes is often transient, as models evolve rapidly and applications shift. Control over inputs, by contrast, shapes who can participate, adapt, and innovate over time. By emphasizing shared infrastructure and public-interest models, India seeks to prevent a future in which advanced technological capability is concentrated within a narrow set of actors whose commercial or strategic priorities may not align with domestic needs.

Architectural autonomy is not costless. Open systems require sustained governance, security investment, and coordination across institutions. They may evolve more slowly than closed platforms optimized for rapid deployment. These trade-offs are accepted because the alternative—digital enclosure—would restrict the ability to adapt as technologies and risks evolve.

For citizens and institutions, the significance of this approach is not always visible. When systems work, their design recedes into the background. Yet it is precisely this background architecture that determines whether a state retains control over its administrative functions during periods of geopolitical tension.

Strategic autonomy in technology, therefore, is not about technological independence in isolation. It is about ensuring that the state's core functions cannot be externally disabled, coerced, or conditioned. By embedding autonomy in standards and systems rather than proclamations, India preserves freedom of judgment in domains that increasingly shape economic and political life.

This architectural understanding of autonomy prepares the ground for the next chapter, where the implications of digital infrastructure and data governance are examined more directly.

## 5.7 Costs, Trade-offs, and Misreadings

Strategic autonomy is often presented as a prudent or cautious posture. In practice, it is demanding. Preserving choice in a transactional world imposes real costs, many of which are visible in the pace and texture of India's external engagements. Autonomy is not the path of least resistance; it is a commitment to managing complexity rather than simplifying it away.

One cost is speed. Alignment can accelerate decisions by outsourcing judgment to alliance structures or predefined commitments. Strategic autonomy requires independent assessment, negotiation across multiple channels, and continual recalibration. Agreements may take longer to conclude. Positions may evolve as conditions change. This "speed tax" is a direct consequence of refusing binary commitments.

Another cost is interpretive friction. Partners accustomed to loyalty-based frameworks may find autonomy unsettling. When expectations are shaped by alignment, flexibility can appear evasive. India's willingness to cooperate intensely in one domain while declining convergence in another is sometimes misread as inconsistency. In reality, it reflects issue-specific evaluation rather than shifting intent.

There are also coordination costs within the state. Strategic autonomy demands institutional coherence across ministries, regulatory bodies, and diplomatic channels. Economic, security, and technological decisions must reinforce rather than undermine one another. Without sustained internal coordination, strategic autonomy risks devolving into fragmented decision-making. Maintaining coherence requires administrative capacity and long-term policy discipline.

A further trade-off lies in foregone advantages. Exclusive partnerships can offer short-term benefits—preferential access, faster integration, or stronger signaling. By declining exclusivity, India may accept fewer immediate gains in exchange for longer-term flexibility. These choices can be politically difficult to explain, particularly when benefits are diffuse and costs visible.

The most persistent misreading, however, is the assumption that autonomy signals indecision or lack of will. This interpretation mistakes restraint for hesitation. Strategic autonomy does not avoid choice; it structures choice. Decisions are made with an explicit awareness of their locking effects and with compensating measures to preserve room for adjustment elsewhere.

Autonomy also does not imply equidistance or neutrality in all matters. India does take positions, sometimes firmly. The distinction is that positions are not universalized across domains. Agreement in one area does not compel alignment in another. This selective engagement can appear untidy, but it reflects disciplined management of interdependence.

Understanding these costs is essential to evaluating the strategy honestly. Strategic autonomy is not cost-free insurance. It is an active investment in flexibility, paid for through slower processes, greater interpretive effort, and sustained institutional attention.

The alternative—simplifying choices through rigid alignment—may reduce friction in the short term but increases vulnerability when conditions change. Strategic autonomy accepts present complexity to reduce future constraint. It is a choice to bear manageable costs today in order to avoid irreversible losses tomorrow.

## 5.8 Interpreting Strategic Autonomy Correctly

Strategic autonomy can be difficult to interpret because it resists simple signals. It does not announce itself through doctrines, red lines, or permanent alignments. Its presence is revealed instead through patterns of choice over time. For the observer—whether citizen, professional, or analyst—the task is therefore not to track declarations, but to examine how decisions accumulate.

The most reliable indicator is consistency of method rather than consistency of position. India may say "yes" to one partner and "no" to another on the same day, or cooperate deeply in one domain while holding back in another. Read narrowly, these actions can appear contradictory. Read through the lens of strategic autonomy, they reflect a system maintaining its own center of gravity.

This lens shifts attention from outcomes to structure. The relevant question is not whether India aligns on a particular issue, but whether the decision preserves freedom of judgment under future uncertainty. When policies leave room for adjustment, substitution, or recalibration, they are consistent with autonomy—even if they appear cautious or incremental in the moment.

Strategic autonomy also clarifies the meaning of restraint. Delayed decisions, qualified commitments, or partial participation are often interpreted as hesitation. In this framework, restraint is a way of preventing premature closure. It keeps pathways open while conditions evolve. What appears indecisive in a demand-driven environment may be deliberate sequencing in a choice-preserving one.

Importantly, autonomy does not imply symmetry. India does not respond identically to all partners or pressures, nor does it seek balance for its own sake. Responses vary because contexts vary. What remains stable is the governing logic: avoid irreversible dependence, distribute risk, and retain the ability to act independently when required.

For readers navigating a constant flow of global news, this perspective offers a practical filter. Rather than reacting to individual headlines or episodic tensions, attention should be paid to whether India's actions narrow or widen its future options. Over time, this pattern becomes visible even when individual decisions appear opaque.

Strategic autonomy, interpreted correctly, is neither evasive nor passive. It is a disciplined approach to governing interdependence in an environment where certainty has eroded. Understanding it requires patience, but it rewards that patience with coherence.

## Chapter Conclusion

Strategic autonomy, as developed in this chapter, is best understood as a method rather than a position. It is not a rejection of engagement, nor a claim of exceptionalism. It is a disciplined approach to preserving freedom of judgment in a global environment where commitments are conditional, systems are interdependent, and leverage is increasingly embedded in infrastructure rather than treaties.

This logic connects directly to the themes established earlier in the book. The civilizational time horizons discussed in Chapter 2 explain why India resists irreversible commitments that compress future choice. The rule-proposing behavior examined in Chapter 3 shows how India seeks to shape systems without imposing doctrine. The multi-alignment strategy explored in Chapter 4 demonstrates how autonomy is operationalized through diversified engagement rather than fixed camps. Strategic autonomy provides the connective tissue among these approaches.

What distinguishes strategic autonomy from earlier formulations is not its ambition, but its realism. It accepts that dependence cannot be eliminated, only managed. It recognizes that alignment can simplify decisions in the short term while narrowing options in the long term. And it treats flexibility not as weakness, but as a form of strength in an uncertain world.

In a fragmented and uncertain global environment, no governing approach offers guaranteed outcomes. Strategic autonomy, in particular, demands institutional capacity, internal coordination, and tolerance for ambiguity. It may slow decisions and complicate partnerships. Yet the alternative—premature closure in a fragmented system—carries risks that are far more difficult to reverse.

Strategic autonomy therefore functions as a governing logic for continuity under change. It allows India to participate fully in global systems while retaining the ability to adapt as those systems evolve. In doing so, it preserves not only policy choice, but the capacity to learn, recalibrate, and endure.

The next chapter turns to the domain where this logic is increasingly tested: digital infrastructure, data governance, and the emerging architectures of power. There, autonomy is no longer abstract. It is built into code, standards, and systems that quietly shape the limits of governance itself.

# Chapter 6: Digital Governance, Data, and Sovereignty

This chapter examines how India's approach to digital governance, data, and participation in the global AI economy together constitute a distinct model of digital statecraft. Rather than treating digital systems as neutral tools or commercial platforms, India approaches them as foundational governance infrastructure. Digital sovereignty, in this view, is not about isolation or control for its own sake, but about preserving the capacity to govern critical systems without external dependency.

The chapter builds on the logic developed in earlier sections of the book. Strategic autonomy, rule-proposing behavior, and multi-alignment all find their most concrete expression in the digital domain. Code, standards, and system design now shape the limits of policy choice as decisively as treaties once did. Understanding India's digital choices therefore provides a practical lens into how autonomy is embedded in everyday governance rather than asserted through declarations.

This chapter is not a catalogue of technologies or initiatives. It focuses instead on governing logic: how systems are designed, who controls them, and how resilience is built into their architecture. The aim is to explain how India seeks to remain digitally integrated with the world while ensuring that its core administrative and economic functions remain subject to domestic judgment and law.

## 6.1 From E-Government to Digital Statecraft

India's early engagement with digital governance followed a familiar trajectory. Initial efforts focused on digitizing existing processes: moving paper records online, automating service delivery, and improving administrative efficiency. These initiatives reduced friction and expanded access, but they largely replicated pre-digital silos in electronic form. Technology was an enabler, not a rethinking of governance itself.

Over time, the limits of this approach became apparent. Digitized silos could improve service delivery, but they did not fundamentally alter how systems interacted or scaled. As the demands of population-scale governance grew, incremental digitization proved insufficient. What was required was not faster processes, but a different underlying logic.

The shift that followed was conceptual rather than technological. India began to treat certain digital functions—identity, payments, authentication, and data exchange—not as applications layered onto governance, but as foundational infrastructure. Much like roads or electricity grids, these systems were designed to be neutral, universally accessible, and governed in the public interest. Their purpose was to enable other services, public and private, rather than to compete with them.

This marks the transition from e-government to digital statecraft. In digital statecraft, technology choices are inseparable from questions of sovereignty, resilience, and public authority. Design decisions determine who can participate, who sets the rules, and how failures propagate. Governance is exercised not only through policy, but through architecture.

A defining feature of this approach is the separation of governance logic from commercial incentives. Digital identity and payment systems are treated as national assets rather than profit centers. This does not exclude private innovation. Instead, it establishes a stable public layer on which innovation can occur without allowing gatekeeping power to concentrate in a few actors.

Digital statecraft also reflects a recognition that scale changes risk. Systems that serve hundreds of millions—or more—cannot be governed in the same way as niche platforms. Security failures, vendor dependency, or legal ambiguity at that scale have systemic consequences. The emphasis therefore shifts from speed and novelty to robustness, auditability, and legal clarity.

This evolution sets the foundation for the sections that follow. India's Digital Public Infrastructure, data governance framework, and approach to emerging technologies all flow from this underlying shift in how digital systems are understood. The question is no longer how to digitize governance, but how to govern the digital domain itself.

## 6.2 Digital Public Infrastructure as a Sovereign Layer

India's Digital Public Infrastructure (DPI) represents a deliberate departure from platform-centric models of digital governance. Rather than building monolithic applications owned by the state or outsourcing core functions to private intermediaries, India has focused on creating a neutral, interoperable layer that sits beneath both public and private services. This layer does not compete with markets. It enables them.

At the core of this approach is a simple design choice: separate foundational functions from end-user applications. Identity, authentication, payments, and document exchange are treated as shared utilities rather than proprietary services. This separation reduces concentration of power, limits gatekeeping, and allows multiple actors to innovate without controlling the underlying system.

The architecture commonly referred to as the "India Stack" reflects this logic. Identity verification, payment authorization, and data exchange are modular and loosely coupled. Each function can evolve independently, and no single component monopolizes the system. This modularity is not merely a technical preference. It is a governance choice that limits dependency and preserves optionality over time.

By design, DPI systems are interoperable. They allow domestic systems to integrate with global networks while remaining governed by domestic law and oversight. This is a critical distinction. Integration does not require surrendering administrative control to external vendors or opaque software regimes. The system remains auditable, adaptable, and subject to public accountability.

This approach also addresses a common risk in digital transformation: monopoly gatekeeping. When foundational digital functions are controlled by a small number of private platforms, access becomes conditional, and governance capacity erodes quietly. DPI prevents this outcome by keeping the core neutral and open, while allowing competition and specialization at the edges.

Importantly, DPI is not framed as a uniquely Indian solution. Its influence flows through utility rather than assertion. The same modular template is being adapted in multiple countries seeking to modernize service delivery without replicating either private monopoly or centralized surveillance models. In these contexts, India is not exporting policy preferences. It is offering a design logic that can be locally governed and modified.

Sovereignty in this model is architectural rather than declarative. It resides in how systems are built, who can modify them, and under which legal jurisdiction they operate.

By embedding governance capacity into the design of digital infrastructure, India reduces the need for reactive controls later. The system itself preserves room for judgment, adaptation, and accountability.

This distinction matters because digital dependence is often invisible until it becomes binding. Once a nation's identity systems, payment rails, or administrative workflows are locked into proprietary regimes, exit becomes costly or impossible. DPI seeks to prevent such enclosure in advance by keeping the foundational layer open, modular, and domestically governed.

Digital Public Infrastructure therefore functions as a sovereign layer not by isolating India from global systems, but by ensuring that integration does not translate into loss of control. It is a preventive form of statecraft, designed to preserve governance capacity under conditions of scale, complexity, and external pressure.

## 6.3 Data as a National Resource Without Centralization

India's approach to data governance reflects a deliberate effort to avoid two dominant models that have emerged elsewhere. One treats data primarily as a commercial asset, accumulated and monetized by private platforms with limited public oversight. The other treats data as a state-held resource, centralized for administrative control and surveillance. India has sought a third path—one that recognizes data as a national resource without concentrating ownership or control in any single actor.

In this model, data sovereignty is not defined by where data physically resides or who collects it, but by the legal and institutional framework under which it is governed. The central question is not accumulation, but agency: who has the right to decide how data is used, shared, and protected.

The Digital Personal Data Protection framework reflects this logic. Rather than asserting blanket state control or deferring entirely to market mechanisms, it anchors data governance in consent, purpose limitation, and accountability. Individuals retain rights over their personal data, while institutions—public and private—are obligated to operate within clearly defined legal boundaries. This creates a regime where data can move, but only under rules that are enforceable within domestic jurisdiction.

This approach is reinforced by India's broader data architecture, particularly the Data Empowerment and Protection Architecture (DEPA). DEPA reframes data sharing as a user-mediated process rather than an institutional transaction. Data does not permanently change hands. Instead, individuals authorize time-bound, purpose-specific access through standardized consent mechanisms. This allows data to circulate across sectors such as finance and health without being centralized into a single repository.

The significance of this design lies in what it prevents. Centralized data systems, whether corporate or state-controlled, tend to create irreversible dependencies. Once data is aggregated and locked into proprietary formats or opaque administrative structures, exit becomes difficult and oversight weakens. India's layered approach avoids this by separating data ownership, data access, and data use, allowing each to be governed independently.

Crucially, this model does not seek to isolate India from global data flows. Cross-border data exchange remains possible, but it is conditioned by domestic law and reciprocal safeguards. Sovereignty, in this sense, is exercised through jurisdiction and enforceability rather than exclusion. Sensitive information remains subject to Indian legal processes even as it participates in global systems.

Treating data as a national resource therefore does not imply nationalization. It implies stewardship. The state's role is to define the rules of use, protect individual rights, and ensure that no single entity—public or private—can unilaterally control access to information that underpins economic activity and governance.

This framing becomes increasingly important as data-driven systems scale. When data underlies credit decisions, welfare delivery, healthcare access, and emerging technologies, governance failures have systemic consequences. India's approach seeks to manage this risk by embedding choice, consent, and legal clarity into the architecture itself.

In doing so, India advances a model of data sovereignty that prioritizes agency over accumulation and governance over control. It is a model designed to remain flexible under pressure, allowing integration with global systems while preserving the capacity to govern data in the public interest.

## 6.4 Participation in the Global AI Economy

India's approach to artificial intelligence reflects the same governing logic that shapes its broader digital strategy. Rather than framing AI as a contest for dominance or a race to deploy the most advanced models, India approaches it as a question of access, capacity, and long-term resilience. The objective is not to control outcomes, but to ensure that participation in the global AI economy does not create new forms of dependency.

Artificial intelligence amplifies existing asymmetries. Access to compute, high-quality data, and skilled talent increasingly determines who can build, deploy, and benefit from AI systems. When these inputs are concentrated in a small number of countries or firms, technological capability becomes conditional rather than broadly accessible. India's strategy seeks to prevent this concentration from hardening into structural exclusion.

Public investment in AI infrastructure reflects this concern. By focusing on shared compute capacity, data resources, and research platforms, India aims to ensure that domestic researchers, startups, and public institutions are not forced to rely exclusively on external providers whose priorities may shift. This is not an attempt to create a self-contained AI ecosystem. It is an effort to maintain bargaining power and continuity in an environment where access can be restricted without warning.

India's role as a convening actor in global AI discussions follows the same pattern. Rather than positioning itself as a regulator imposing standards, India has emphasized capacity-building, safety, and access. Forums such as the India AI Impact Summit have focused on lowering entry barriers for developing countries by highlighting shared datasets, public-interest models, and cooperative research frameworks. The emphasis is on widening participation rather than narrowing control.

This approach reflects an understanding that AI governance cannot be reduced to a binary choice between regulation and innovation. Excessive regulatory rigidity can stifle development, while unrestrained commercialization can concentrate power and undermine public accountability. India's focus on infrastructure seeks to balance these risks by shaping the conditions under which AI is developed and deployed, rather than dictating outcomes.

Participation in the global AI economy also requires openness. India remains integrated into international research networks, talent flows, and commercial markets. Its universities, startups, and firms collaborate with global partners across multiple jurisdictions. Strategic autonomy in this context does not mean technological separation. It means retaining the ability to choose partners, architectures, and applications without being locked into a single ecosystem.

By emphasizing inputs over outputs, and architecture over assertion, India positions itself as a bridge between advanced AI producers and emerging adopters. This role is not ideological. It is functional. It seeks to ensure that the benefits of AI are not limited to those who control proprietary systems, and that technological capability remains compatible with domestic governance and public interest.

In this sense, India's participation in the global AI economy is an extension of its broader digital statecraft. It is an effort to remain fully engaged while preserving the freedom to govern critical systems under conditions of rapid technological change.

## 6.5 Standards, Interfaces, and Power

As digital systems mature, power increasingly flows through standards rather than through ownership of applications or platforms. Technical specifications, interoperability rules, and interface definitions quietly determine who can participate, on what terms, and at what cost. In this environment, influence is exercised upstream, long before policy disputes or market competition become visible.

Standards bodies are often perceived as technical forums removed from geopolitics. In practice, they are among the most consequential arenas of contemporary statecraft. Decisions made in these settings shape market access, technological pathways, and regulatory constraints for decades. Once standards are widely adopted, they become difficult to dislodge, even when they embed asymmetries or dependencies.

India's engagement with standards reflects a clear recognition of this dynamic. Rather than treating standards as neutral technical outcomes to be accepted after the fact, India seeks early and sustained presence in their formulation. The objective is not to dominate proceedings or impose national preferences, but to ensure that emerging standards remain interoperable, adaptable, and compatible with diverse governance models.

This approach aligns with India's broader emphasis on modularity and openness. Standards that assume centralized control, proprietary interfaces, or closed ecosystems risk excluding large segments of the global population and locking countries into paths they did not choose. By contrast, open and flexible standards preserve optionality. They allow systems to evolve, integrate, and localize without requiring wholesale replacement.

Participation in standards-setting also serves a risk-management function. When standards are written without India's input, the cost of later compliance can be high. Retrofitting domestic systems to externally defined rules often requires policy concessions, financial outlays, or loss of control over core functions. Early engagement reduces these risks by shaping the design space itself.

Importantly, India's approach to standards does not rely on volume or leverage alone. It draws credibility from operational experience. Systems built at population scale generate insights that purely theoretical frameworks cannot. This practical grounding allows India to contribute constructively to discussions on interoperability, security, and governance without resorting to ideological positions.

Standards, interfaces, and protocols therefore represent a quiet but durable form of influence. They define the boundaries within which markets operate and policies are implemented. By remaining present in these processes, India seeks to ensure that future digital ecosystems remain plural rather than consolidated, and that governance capacity is preserved even as systems globalize.

In this sense, standards work is not ancillary to digital sovereignty. It is one of its primary instruments. Power exercised through design endures longer, travels further, and provokes less resistance than power asserted through declaration.

## 6.6 Risks of Digital Enclosure and Dependency

As digital systems become foundational to governance and economic activity, new forms of dependency emerge that are less visible than traditional supply-chain vulnerabilities. One of the most significant is digital enclosure: a condition in which a nation's core administrative or economic systems become tightly coupled to a small number of external providers, platforms, or proprietary technologies. Once established, such dependence can quietly erode strategic autonomy without triggering immediate policy debate.

Digital enclosure does not require coercion. It often arises through convenience, speed, or short-term efficiency gains. Proprietary systems promise rapid deployment, seamless integration, and reduced upfront costs. Over time, however, these benefits can give way to structural lock-in. When upgrades, security patches, pricing, or access conditions are controlled externally, domestic authorities lose effective control over systems that are essential to daily governance.

The risk is magnified at scale. When identity verification, payments, public records, or communications infrastructure depend on closed systems, the consequences of disruption extend far beyond individual services. A contractual dispute, regulatory change in another jurisdiction, or unilateral platform decision can propagate into systemic failure. In such cases, formal sovereignty remains intact, but operational autonomy is diminished.

India's digital strategy seeks to address this risk through preventive design. By prioritizing open standards, interoperability, and auditability, it reduces reliance on opaque "black box" technologies whose internal workings and decision rules are inaccessible. Free and open-source software, modular architectures, and vendor diversity are treated not merely as technical preferences, but as safeguards against enclosure.

This approach does not reject private participation. Private firms play a critical role in innovation, service delivery, and system improvement. The distinction lies in control over the foundational layer. When core systems remain open and governed by public rules, private actors compete on services rather than on access. This preserves flexibility and limits the accumulation of unaccountable power.

Preventing digital enclosure also has long-term fiscal and security implications. Exit costs from proprietary systems tend to rise over time, making course correction politically and economically difficult. By contrast, open architectures preserve the option to adapt, replace components, or shift partners as conditions change. This optionality is central to maintaining autonomy in a rapidly evolving technological landscape.

The focus on avoiding digital enclosure reflects a broader principle of India's digital statecraft. Structural risks are those that arise from how systems are built—dependencies that become difficult to reverse once embedded in everyday operations. When reliance on external technologies becomes routine, the scope for policy adjustment shrinks. Embedding resilience into digital architecture is therefore a way to protect governance capacity under conditions of technological or geopolitical stress.

Digital enclosure, in this sense, is not a hypothetical threat. It is a structural risk inherent in contemporary digital transformation. India's approach treats it as such, addressing it through architecture and governance rather than through reactive regulation.

## 6.7 Costs, Trade-offs, and Governance Burdens

The digital governance model described in this chapter is not without cost. Open, modular, and interoperable systems demand sustained institutional capacity. They require coordination across ministries, regulators, technologists, and legal authorities. Unlike proprietary systems that centralize responsibility in a single vendor, public digital infrastructure distributes responsibility across the state. This distribution increases resilience, but it also increases the burden of governance.

One of the most visible costs is operational complexity. Systems designed to serve at population scale must remain secure, reliable, and continuously available. As transaction volumes rise, so do the consequences of failure. Security-by-design becomes a necessity rather than a preference. This requires ongoing investment in monitoring, audits, redundancy, and incident response, often without the immediate efficiencies promised by closed systems.

There is also a trade-off between speed and durability. Proprietary solutions can often be deployed quickly, offering polished interfaces and rapid scaling. Modular public systems evolve more gradually. They require consultation, testing, and consensus-building. In the short term, this can slow deployment and frustrate stakeholders accustomed to faster timelines. Over time, however, the same features that slow initial rollout enable adaptation and correction without wholesale replacement.

Governance burden also manifests in regulatory complexity. Open systems demand clear rules around access, liability, privacy, and accountability. These rules must be updated as technology evolves, without undermining trust or stability. The work of governance does not end with deployment; it becomes continuous. This persistence can strain administrative capacity, particularly when multiple systems interact across sectors.

There is, finally, an interpretive cost. Open digital architectures are often misread by external observers. The absence of a single controlling authority can appear as fragmentation. The refusal to adopt closed platforms may be interpreted as hesitation or lack of ambition. Managing these perceptions requires sustained explanation and diplomatic effort, especially in environments that favor clear alignment or singular control.

Without sustained internal coordination, autonomy can erode into incoherence. Modular systems depend on shared standards, disciplined implementation, and institutional alignment. When coordination weakens, the advantages of openness diminish. The challenge, therefore, is not merely to build open systems, but to govern them effectively over time.

These costs are real, and they accumulate. Yet they are incurred deliberately. The alternative—convenience-driven dependence on closed systems—offers speed at the expense of long-term control. India's digital statecraft accepts higher governance burden as the price of preserving choice, adaptability, and authority in an increasingly inter-connected digital environment.

## 6.8 Interpreting India's Digital Sovereignty Model

Interpreting India's digital choices requires a shift in where attention is placed. The most important signals are not found in declarations, slogans, or isolated policy announcements. They are found in architecture. The question is not whether India claims sovereignty, but how its systems are designed to preserve it.

A useful mental model is to distinguish between walls and bridges. Walls isolate. They limit exposure but also restrict exchange and adaptation. Bridges, by contrast, allow movement while preserving structure. India's digital governance model consistently favors bridges: interoperable systems, open standards, and layered architectures that connect domestic systems to global networks without surrendering control.

This emphasis on architecture over assertion explains why India often appears restrained in its digital diplomacy. It does not seek to impose universal rules or export regulatory frameworks wholesale. Instead, it focuses on ensuring that its own systems—and those that choose to adopt similar templates—remain adaptable, auditable, and governed under transparent legal regimes.

For the observer, the task is to look for consistency of design rather than uniformity of position. When India resists closed platforms, emphasizes interoperability, or invests in shared infrastructure, these are not isolated technical decisions. They reflect a coherent approach to preserving governance capacity in an environment where digital systems increasingly shape economic and political outcomes.

Understanding this model also helps clarify apparent contradictions. Openness to global participation coexists with insistence on domestic legal jurisdiction. Collaboration with private firms proceeds alongside resistance to monopoly gatekeeping. These are not tensions to be resolved. They are features of a system designed to balance integration with autonomy.

Digital sovereignty, in this sense, is not a static condition. It is a continuous practice. It depends on vigilance, institutional capacity, and the willingness to bear governance costs in exchange for long-term flexibility. India's approach treats these costs as investments rather than inefficiencies.

Seen in comparative terms, India's digital sovereignty model differs not by ambition but by design logic. A fuller illustrative comparison of these design approaches is provided in Appendix A for readers who wish to explore them in greater detail. In some systems, core digital functions such as identity, payments, or cloud services are mediated primarily by private platforms. Public authority is exercised later, through regulation, after scale and dependency have already formed. In others, these same functions are centralized within government systems, prioritizing administrative control and uniformity. India's approach is infrastructure-centric. Identity verification, payment rails, and data exchange are treated as public utilities—available to all participants on equal terms—while banks, startups, and service providers compete at the higher, or application layer. Governance is exercised through standards, consent frameworks, and legal jurisdiction rather than through ownership or exclusion. The distinction is practical rather than ideological: it reflects an attempt to preserve adaptability and public authority in systems that must operate at national scale over long time horizons.

## Chapter Conclusion

Digital governance has become one of the primary arenas in which strategic autonomy is exercised. Decisions embedded in code, standards, and system architecture now shape policy options as decisively as formal agreements once did. India's approach reflects a recognition that sovereignty in the digital age must be built into everyday systems rather than asserted episodically.

By treating digital identity, payments, data exchange, and emerging technologies as public-interest infrastructure, India seeks to remain fully integrated with the global digital economy while preserving the capacity to govern critical functions under domestic law. This is neither technological isolation nor regulatory dominance. It is an effort to ensure that participation does not translate into dependency.

The model carries costs. It demands coordination, sustained investment, and tolerance for complexity. It can be slower and less visible than centralized alternatives. Yet it preserves something that is increasingly scarce in a fragmented digital environment: the freedom to adapt, correct, and choose.

In embedding autonomy within architecture, India reduces the need for reactive controls later. Governance capacity is preserved not through exclusion, but through design. As digital systems continue to reshape economic and political life, this preventive approach to sovereignty offers a durable way to manage integration without surrendering judgment.

This chapter completes the book's treatment of autonomy at the level where it now matters most. What follows will examine how these architectural choices interact with global institutions, economic leverage, and the broader distribution of power in a changing world.

The preceding chapters defined the logic by which India seeks to preserve choice: through modularity, civilizational digestion, and the refusal of binary alignment. However, statecraft does not exist in a vacuum. It is anchored by the physical realities of the subcontinent.

The chapters that follow examine the "Material Triad"—the hardcoded frictions of land, the systemic speed limits of resources, and the external exposure of the sea. Here, logic meets gravity, and the "Long View" is tested against the slow, unyielding realities of the physical world.

# Part II: Material Constraint

# Chapter 7: Land-Based Constraints: The Friction of Geography

India's external strategy cannot be understood independently of its internal geography. Before questions of alignment, autonomy, or global ambition arise, the state must first contend with the physical realities of its landmass. Distance, terrain, and internal fragmentation impose costs that shape what is possible, how quickly change can occur, and where strategic vulnerability accumulates.

This chapter examines land-based infrastructure not as a development narrative or a measure of state capacity, but as a response to persistent geographic friction. Roads, railways, logistics corridors, and border connectivity are treated here as structural countermeasures—tools designed to reduce the cost of distance, delay, and internal disconnection rather than as symbols of progress or national achievement.

Understanding this logic is essential for interpreting India's policy choices. Infrastructure decisions that appear incremental or uneven often reflect the scale and complexity of the terrain being addressed. Geography functions not as destiny, but as a "constant variable," one whose parameters do not change for a given country, even as the strategies built around it must. This chapter sets the foundation for the discussion that follows by showing how physical constraints shape India's economic integration, regional posture, and long-term autonomy.

## 7.1 Geography as a Strategic Constraint

If the preceding chapters defined the logic of the Sovereign Pole, this chapter defines its anchor. While geography does not change, the ways states interpret and act upon its constraints and opportunities necessarily do. Before questions of autonomy or multi-alignment reach the cabinet table, they must first pass through the filter of physical friction. These frictions are not incidental. They are embedded in the land itself and continue to influence contemporary trade patterns, regional disparities, and strategic vulnerabilities.

For India, three features are particularly consequential.

To the north, the Himalayan range forms one of the world's most formidable natural barriers. While it provides a measure of strategic insulation, it also limits overland connectivity with Central Asia and constrains the movement of goods, energy, and people. Mountain terrain raises costs, slows infrastructure deployment, and concentrates access along a narrow set of corridors that are difficult to expand or duplicate. This makes northern connectivity inherently fragile and sensitive to disruption.

Across the interior, the Deccan plateau introduces a different form of friction. Its rugged terrain, variable elevation, and dispersed settlement patterns complicate the creation of seamless transport networks. Movement across the plateau is not impossible, but it is expensive. Roads and railways must contend with geological complexity, land fragmentation, and uneven population density. As a result, economic integration across large portions of the interior has historically lagged behind coastal regions.

Finally, India's sheer internal scale creates distance-based friction even where terrain is relatively flat. Resource-rich interiors—coal belts, mineral zones, agricultural regions—are often far from consumption centers and ports. The cost of moving bulk goods across long distances, through congested or incomplete networks, has acted as a persistent brake on industrial competitiveness. Over time, this has contributed to a familiar pattern: coastal regions integrate more rapidly into global trade, while landlocked regions face structural disadvantages.

This internal geography produces a strategic dilemma. Left unattended, it encourages divergence—between coast and interior, between connected and disconnected regions, and between globally integrated enclaves and domestic peripheries. Such divergence is not merely an economic issue. It carries political and strategic consequences, weakening national coherence and increasing the cost of governance.

The response, therefore, cannot be occasional or symbolic. It has to be sustained and systematic. Reducing the cost of distance becomes a core function of the state, not because geography can be defeated, but because its effects can be managed. In this context, infrastructure is less about speed or spectacle and more about continuity—making sure that goods, labor, and opportunity can move reliably across a large and uneven landmass.

Seen through this lens, India's infrastructure efforts reflect an enduring strategic logic. They seek to reduce geography's tendency to pull regions apart and to maintain the conditions for long-term integration. The objective is not to erase constraint, but to prevent constraint from becoming determinative.

## 7.2 Lowering Friction, Not Chasing Speed

A recurring feature of infrastructure debates is the temptation to equate progress with speed. Faster trains, wider highways, and record-breaking construction timelines often become shorthand for national ambition. While speed has value, it is not the core strategic objective in a country shaped by India's geography and scale. What matters more is whether infrastructure lowers friction across the system as a whole.

India's recent infrastructure push reflects a shift away from isolated, prestige-driven projects toward a more coordinated approach. The emphasis is not on building the fastest asset in a single location, but on reducing bottlenecks that raise costs across supply chains. A road that does not connect to a logistics hub, a port that lacks rail access, or an industrial park without reliable power does little to improve overall efficiency. Speed in one segment cannot compensate for friction elsewhere.

The PM Gati Shakti National Master Plan for Multimodal Connectivity reflects this change in orientation. Its significance lies less in any individual project and more in how projects are conceived. By integrating multiple layers of geospatial and administrative data, the framework forces coordination across ministries and jurisdictions that traditionally operated in silos. Infrastructure planning becomes a shared exercise rather than a collection of parallel efforts.

This approach treats infrastructure as a system rather than a set of assets. A highway is evaluated not only for how quickly it can be built, but for how it links to ports, freight terminals, industrial clusters, and urban centers. Rail lines are assessed not only for their passenger service or public visibility, but for how effectively they move freight and connect products to markets. The objective is to ensure that each investment reduces friction somewhere in the network, rather than adding capacity in isolation.

The focus on friction reduction also explains why many projects appear incremental rather than dramatic. Improving logistics efficiency often involves small, unglamorous interventions: grade separations, last-mile links, multimodal parks, or better coordination between agencies. These changes rarely attract attention, but their cumulative effect is substantial. Over time, they lower the cost of moving goods and people, which directly affects competitiveness and growth.

Seen this way, infrastructure is not primarily a signal of state capacity or political will. It is a form of economic housekeeping. The gains come not from speed alone, but from reliability, predictability, and integration. By prioritizing coordination over spectacle, India is attempting to address the deeper sources of friction that have historically limited internal integration.

This shift matters because it aligns infrastructure policy with long-term strategic needs. Reducing friction strengthens domestic cohesion, supports manufacturing and trade, and lowers vulnerability to external shocks. The aim is not to outrun geography, but to work within its constraints in a disciplined and repeatable way.

## 7.3 Internal Connectivity and Economic Integration

Lowering geographic friction is not only about moving goods and people faster; it is about reshaping where economic activity can occur. In India's case, weak internal connectivity has historically reinforced regional concentration. Manufacturing and services gravitated toward coastal cities and a limited number of urban hubs, while large parts of the interior remained poorly integrated into national and global markets. This pattern was not simply a function of policy preference. It reflected the high cost of distance within the country.

Internal connectivity initiatives such as the Dedicated Freight Corridors and the Industrial Corridor Programme are best understood as responses to this structural imbalance. Their objective is not to create isolated zones of excellence, but to make production viable across a wider geography. By separating freight from passenger traffic and providing predictable, high-capacity logistics routes, these corridors reduce uncertainty for manufacturers whose margins depend on reliability rather than speed alone.

The Dedicated Freight Corridors, in particular, address a long-standing constraint. When freight competes with passenger traffic on the same rail network, delays compound and planning becomes difficult. Dedicated lines allow cargo movement to be scheduled with greater certainty, lowering inventory costs and reducing dependence on road transport. The strategic effect is subtle but significant: it changes the economics of location. Firms no longer need to cluster exclusively near ports or major metros to remain competitive.

Industrial corridors extend this logic further. Rather than dispersing infrastructure thinly across the country, they concentrate investment along defined axes that combine transport, power, water, and urban services. This clustering lowers entry barriers for firms that cannot afford to build these systems independently. For smaller manufacturers and suppliers, access to shared infrastructure can determine whether participation in national supply chains is feasible at all.

This approach also speaks directly to the risk of middle-income stagnation. Sustained growth requires expanding the base of productive employment, particularly in manufacturing and logistics-intensive sectors. That expansion is difficult if economic activity remains confined to a narrow set of locations. By enabling industrial activity in tier-two cities and interior regions, internal connectivity becomes a tool for broadening growth rather than merely accelerating it.

Importantly, these efforts do not eliminate regional disparities overnight. Connectivity reduces friction; it does not erase differences in skills, capital availability, or governance quality. But by lowering the structural costs that previously excluded large regions from economic participation, internal integration creates the conditions under which convergence becomes possible over time.

Seen in this light, internal connectivity is not simply an economic policy. It is a strategic investment in national coherence. When regions are better connected to markets, supply chains, and opportunity, the state's ability to manage economic shocks and social pressures improves. Integration strengthens resilience, not by centralizing activity, but by widening the set of regions that can contribute to and benefit from growth.

## 7.4 Regional Connectivity and Strategic Geography

India's land-based constraints do not end at its borders. In fact, many of the most consequential frictions arise precisely at the points where domestic infrastructure meets regional geography. Borders with difficult terrain, unstable neighbors, or limited transit access amplify the cost of distance and restrict India's options for trade and energy flows. Managing these constraints requires a form of connectivity that is both economic and strategic.

Regional connectivity initiatives are often misread as expressions of influence or competition. A more accurate interpretation is that they reflect an effort to limit how much geography can restrict India's options. When overland routes are constrained by political instability or physical barriers, the state must look for alternative pathways that reduce exposure to disruption. Connectivity, in this sense, is less about expansion and more about insulation.

The India–Middle East–Europe Economic Corridor illustrates this logic. Rather than framing it as a rival to existing routes or as a statement of alignment, it is better understood as a form of system insurance. By creating a parallel trade and logistics pathway, India reduces its dependence on a narrow set of maritime chokepoints and overland corridors that are vulnerable to congestion, conflict, or political leverage. The strategic value lies not in replacing existing routes, but in ensuring that no single route becomes indispensable.

A similar logic applies to border infrastructure along India's northern and eastern frontiers. Roads, tunnels, and logistics nodes in difficult terrain are not primarily about rapid mobilization or symbolic presence. They address a more basic requirement: maintaining viable access to regions where geography and climate impose natural limits. Improved connectivity allows civilian supply chains, emergency services, and economic activity to function with greater reliability, reducing the sense of isolation that often accompanies peripheral regions.

These investments also reflect a broader shift in how regional engagement is conceived. Rather than treating borders as static lines of separation, connectivity efforts treat them as zones where friction can either accumulate or be reduced. Better infrastructure does not dissolve political tensions, but it lowers the cost of managing them. It enables calibrated responses instead of reactive ones, and sustained presence instead of episodic intervention.

Importantly, regional connectivity does not imply uniform openness. Choices about routes, partners, and sequencing remain selective. The objective is not to maximise exposure, but to preserve optionality. Multiple pathways—whether through land, sea, or hybrid corridors—allow India to adjust to changing regional conditions without abrupt disruption to trade or supply chains.

This approach aligns with the broader theme of strategic autonomy developed earlier in the book. Autonomy, in this context, is not achieved by withdrawing from regional systems, nor by binding oneself to a single framework. It is achieved by ensuring that engagement is diversified and resilient. Connectivity becomes a tool for managing dependence rather than eliminating it.

Seen through this lens, regional infrastructure initiatives are less about ambition than about risk management. They are attempts to stabilize India's interaction with its neighborhood by reducing the leverage that geography and instability can exert. By investing in alternative routes and redundant connections, India seeks to ensure that regional shocks do not cascade into domestic disruption.

Regional connectivity, therefore, is not an outward projection of power. It is an inward-facing strategy aimed at protecting the integrity of domestic economic and social systems. The emphasis is on continuity rather than control, and on flexibility rather than dominance. Geography may set the boundaries of possibility, but connectivity determines how tightly those boundaries constrain national choice.

## 7.5 Infrastructure, Autonomy, and Choice Preservation

Physical infrastructure plays a quiet but decisive role in preserving national choice. While debates about autonomy often focus on diplomacy, trade policy, or security arrangements, the ability to act independently is frequently shaped by more basic factors: how easily goods can move within the country, how many routes exist to reach markets, and how vulnerable supply chains are to disruption.

From this perspective, infrastructure is not simply an enabler of growth. It is a hedge against constraint. Each additional logistics corridor, multimodal terminal, or secondary port reduces the degree to which any single route, region, or external event can exert outsized influence on the domestic economy. Autonomy is strengthened not through isolation, but through redundancy.

This logic mirrors the broader principle of choice preservation discussed earlier in the book. A system with multiple pathways can absorb shocks without forcing abrupt or irreversible decisions. When transport networks are sparse or concentrated, even minor disruptions can create cascading effects that narrow policy options. Governments are then compelled to respond defensively, prioritizing short-term stabilization over longer-term judgment.

Infrastructure investment, in this sense, expands the range of feasible responses. It allows economic activity to be rerouted, supply chains to be reconfigured, and regional imbalances to be managed with greater flexibility. The strategic value lies not in preventing disruption altogether, but in ensuring that disruption does not dictate outcomes.

This also helps explain why many infrastructure decisions appear cautious or incremental. Building redundancy is rarely dramatic. It involves parallel routes, backup capacity, and investments whose value becomes apparent only under stress. These choices may seem inefficient in periods of stability, but they reduce vulnerability when conditions deteriorate. In strategic terms, they function as insurance.

Importantly, this approach avoids framing infrastructure as a zero-sum contest. Reducing dependence on a single corridor or chokepoint does not imply hostility toward existing partners or routes. It reflects a preference for resilience over reliance. By ensuring that no single pathway becomes indispensable, India preserves the freedom to adjust its economic and strategic posture without coercion.

Infrastructure-led autonomy also has domestic implications. Regions that are better connected to national markets are less exposed to localized shocks and political pressure. Economic diversification becomes easier, and governance responses can be calibrated rather than reactive. In this way, physical connectivity reinforces institutional stability as much as economic performance.

Seen in this light, infrastructure is a foundational layer of strategic autonomy. It does not determine policy outcomes, but it shapes the space within which policy choices can be made. By lowering internal friction and creating alternative routes for trade and movement, India reduces the risk that external or internal disruptions force premature or constrained decisions.

Choice preservation, therefore, is not an abstract principle. It is built into roads, railways, ports, and logistics systems that quietly expand the country's room for maneuver. Infrastructure becomes a means of keeping options open—an investment in flexibility that pays dividends over time, especially in an increasingly uncertain global environment.

## 7.6 Execution Constraints and Trade-offs

Infrastructure strategy is ultimately tested not in planning documents but in execution. In India's case, the gap between intent and outcome is shaped by constraints that are structural rather than episodic. Geography sets the baseline, but law, institutions, and social complexity determine how quickly and consistently that geography can be managed.

Land acquisition remains the most persistent constraint. Infrastructure corridors necessarily cut across densely inhabited and legally fragmented landscapes. Property rights, environmental clearances, and local consent are not procedural obstacles that can be bypassed; they are features of a democratic system governing a large and diverse society. Delays that appear inefficient from the outside often reflect the time required to reconcile competing claims over land, livelihood, and compensation.

Federal complexity adds another layer of friction. Transport and logistics projects routinely span multiple states and jurisdictions, each with distinct priorities and administrative capacities. Coordination across these layers is costly in time and political capital. Central planning can align incentives, but it cannot eliminate the need for negotiation and compromise at the local level. As a result, progress is often uneven, advancing faster in some regions than others.

There are also financial trade-offs. Sustained investment in infrastructure requires high levels of public expenditure over long periods, often before visible returns materialize. This creates tension with other fiscal priorities, particularly social spending and debt management. Choices must be made not only about what to build, but about sequencing and scale. Redundancy improves resilience, but it also raises upfront costs.

These constraints do not negate the strategic logic of infrastructure investment. They shape its tempo. In a system of this scale, continuity matters more than acceleration. Sudden surges followed by long pauses tend to increase inefficiency and erode institutional learning. Gradual, sustained execution allows agencies to adapt, coordinate, and correct course over time.

Importantly, execution limits also impose discipline. They force prioritization and prevent overextension. Not every corridor can be built at once, and not every bottleneck can be addressed simultaneously. Strategic clarity lies in choosing which frictions matter most and allocating resources accordingly. This selectivity is a feature, not a failure.

Understanding these trade-offs is essential for interpreting infrastructure outcomes. Delays do not automatically signal lack of intent, just as rapid progress does not guarantee long-term effectiveness. What matters is whether investments continue to reduce friction incrementally and whether institutions retain the capacity to carry projects forward across political cycles.

In this sense, execution constraints are not merely obstacles to be overcome. They are conditions that shape how infrastructure strategy unfolds in practice. Managing them requires patience, coordination, and tolerance for imperfection—qualities that are often undervalued, but indispensable when geography and scale cannot be wished away.

## 7.7 Interpreting Infrastructure Signals

Infrastructure attracts attention because it is visible. New highways, rail lines, ports, and corridors lend themselves easily to political messaging and media coverage. For the observer, however, visibility is a poor guide to strategic significance. The more useful question is not how large or fast a project appears, but what kind of constraint it addresses.

A helpful way to read infrastructure signals is to distinguish between expansion and redundancy. Projects that add capacity along a single route may improve throughput, but they also concentrate dependence. By contrast, projects that create alternative pathways—parallel rail lines, secondary ports, multimodal links, or bypasses—reduce vulnerability even if they do not immediately transform headline statistics. Strategic value often lies in the second category.

Another useful test is to ask whether a project lowers friction across the system or only within a narrow segment. An isolated asset, however impressive, does little if it remains disconnected from supply chains, markets, or logistics hubs. Infrastructure that links production zones to ports, or inland regions to multiple gateways, has effects that compound over time. These projects rarely attract attention because their impact is distributed rather than dramatic.

Observers should also pay attention to sequencing. Infrastructure that appears modest today may be laying the groundwork for larger shifts later. Freight corridors, logistics parks, and last-mile connections often precede visible industrial activity. Judging such investments prematurely can lead to misinterpretation, especially in systems where returns materialize slowly.

Finally, it is important to separate intention from execution speed. Delays, revisions, and uneven progress are common in large democracies operating across complex legal, social, and institutional environments. They do not necessarily indicate strategic drift. The more reliable signal is continuity of direction: whether successive decisions continue to reduce the same set of frictions over time.

Taken together, these lenses allow readers to look past formal announcements and assess underlying strategic realities. The strategic question is not whether infrastructure is expanding, but whether it is increasing flexibility. Does a new project create another way for goods, energy, or people to move if existing routes are disrupted? Does it reduce dependence on a single corridor, region, or chokepoint?

When infrastructure is read in this way, its role in India's broader strategy becomes clearer. It is not about spectacle or acceleration. It is about quietly widening the space in which choices can be made. That widening, rather than the pace of construction, is the true indicator of strategic intent.

## Chapter Conclusion

India's land-based infrastructure choices are best understood as responses to constraint rather than expressions of ambition. Geography sets limits that cannot be wished away, but it does not dictate outcomes. What matters is how consistently those limits are managed, and whether the costs they impose are allowed to accumulate unchecked or are reduced through sustained effort.

Seen in this light, infrastructure is neither a symbol nor a shortcut. It is a long-term commitment to lowering internal friction so that economic integration, regional balance, and strategic flexibility remain viable over time. Progress is measured not by speed or spectacle, but by whether movement becomes more reliable, alternatives more available, and dependence less concentrated.

This perspective also clarifies why infrastructure outcomes often appear uneven. In a country of India's size, execution reflects legal, social, and institutional complexity as much as engineering capacity. Delays and trade-offs are not deviations from strategy; they are part of how strategy is implemented under democratic constraints.

Most importantly, land-based connectivity reinforces the broader themes of autonomy and choice preservation developed earlier in the book. By creating multiple pathways for goods, people, and resources to move, infrastructure widens the space within which decisions can be made. It reduces the risk that geography, disruption, or external pressure will force premature or constrained choices.

The chapters that follow extend this logic beyond land. Resource security and maritime access pose different constraints, but the governing principle remains the same: strategic resilience is built by managing friction, not denying it.

# Chapter 8: Resource Constraints: Securing the Engine of Growth

Economic growth is not powered by intent alone. It depends on continuous access to energy, materials, and natural inputs that are unevenly distributed and are increasingly contested. For a large, fast-growing economy, these constraints are not temporary challenges to be solved once, but enduring conditions that must be managed across cycles of volatility, transition, and geopolitical stress.

This chapter examines how India approaches resource security not as a pursuit of self-sufficiency or dominance, but as a problem of stability and risk distribution. The focus is on how dependence is structured, buffered, and diversified so that it does not become a source of coercion or a brake on growth. Resource policy, in this sense, is less about achieving an ideal end state and more about preserving continuity under uncertain conditions.

Understanding this logic is essential for interpreting India's choices in energy, climate, and materials. What may appear cautious, contradictory, or incremental often reflects an effort to prevent dependence from hardening into constraint. The aim is not to eliminate exposure, but to ensure that exposure remains manageable, reversible, and subject to domestic judgment.

## 8.1 Resource Dependence as a Structural Reality

For a country of India's size and growth trajectory, resource dependence is not an anomaly—it is a structural condition. Large populations, rising incomes, and expanding industrial capacity require inputs that cannot always be produced domestically at scale or at competitive cost. Attempts to eliminate imports entirely would slow growth, raise prices, and reduce flexibility long before they increased security.

This reality requires a clear distinction between self-sufficiency and the ability to act independently ("sovereign agency"). Self-sufficiency implies the ability to meet demand internally, regardless of cost or efficiency. Sovereign agency, by contrast, refers to the capacity to manage dependence without surrendering control over critical decisions. In practice, this means accepting imports while ensuring that no single source, route, or supplier can exercise undue influence.

A useful way to understand this condition is through the concept of strategic exposure. What matters is not whether a country imports, but whether those imports come from too few sources. Import dependence becomes risky not because it exists, but because it is concentrated. When supplies are diversified, contracts are staggered, and alternatives remain available, exposure is spread across multiple relationships rather than embedded in any one of them. Dependence, in this form, becomes manageable rather than coercive.

India's approach reflects this distinction. Rather than framing imports as a vulnerability to be eliminated, policy is oriented toward shaping the terms under which imports occur. The objective is to ensure continuity of supply across price cycles, geopolitical shifts, and market disruptions. This requires diversification not only of suppliers, but also of transport routes, contract structures, and institutional arrangements.

Importantly, managing dependence is an ongoing process rather than a fixed achievement. Markets evolve, technologies shift, and geopolitical alignments change. What appears diversified at one moment can become concentrated at another. Strategic exposure therefore demands continual adjustment rather than a one-time solution.

Seen in this light, resource dependence is not a failure of policy. It is the baseline condition from which policy operates. The strategic question is not whether India imports resources, but whether those imports narrow or preserve its freedom of action over time. This chapter examines how that logic plays out across energy systems and climate-linked transition pressures.

## 8.2 Energy as a Speed Limit, Not a Sector

Energy is often discussed as a sector of the economy—alongside agriculture, manufacturing, or services. For a fast-growing country, this framing is misleading. Energy availability and pricing act less like a discrete sector and more like a system-wide constraint. They determine how quickly an economy can expand and how resilient it remains under stress.

The central challenge is not absolute scarcity, but volatility. Sudden changes in energy prices function as an immediate tax on households, firms, and the state. When energy costs rise sharply, transport becomes more expensive, manufacturing margins shrink, and inflationary pressures spread across the economy. These effects are rapid and difficult to offset, especially in economies where energy demand continues to grow.

From a strategic perspective, the objective is therefore continuity rather than optimization. Reliable supply and price stability matter more than achieving the lowest possible cost in any given year. An energy system that performs well in normal conditions but fails under stress imposes hidden risks. Conversely, systems designed to absorb shocks may appear less efficient in the short term but provide greater macroeconomic stability over time.

This logic helps explain why India's energy choices often resist simple categorization. The priority is not to privilege one source over another, but to ensure that no single disruption—whether geopolitical, climatic, or market-driven—can significantly slow economic activity. Energy policy, in this sense, functions as a form of shock management.

Energy volatility also has implications beyond economics. Sharp price movements constrain fiscal policy, complicate welfare provision, and limit room for maneuver in external negotiations. When energy costs dominate the policy agenda, other priorities are crowded out. Managing this risk becomes a prerequisite for maintaining strategic focus.

Seen through this lens, debates that reduce energy policy to questions of preference or ideology miss the underlying constraint. For a country still expanding its industrial base and lifting incomes, the binding concern is not the label attached to an energy source, but whether the system as a whole can sustain growth without frequent disruption.

Treating energy as a speed limit rather than a sector shifts attention to resilience. It places emphasis on buffers, diversification, and continuity of supply rather than on singular transitions or end states. This approach does not deny the importance of long-term change. It insists, however, that transition itself must be managed in a way that does not destabilize the engine of growth it depends upon.

## 8.3 Diversification Over Substitution

Energy debates often assume a clean substitution logic: one source replaces another as technology advances or costs fall. In practice, this model rarely holds for large, fast-growing economies. Energy systems do not change by replacement alone; they evolve through layering. India's approach reflects this reality.

The central principle is diversification rather than substitution. No single energy source is expected to carry the full burden of growth, nor is any existing source retired before alternatives have demonstrated reliability at scale. This is not a failure to choose. It is a conscious refusal to concentrate risk.

Coal, for example, continues to provide base-load stability. Its role reflects system requirements, not political preference. It anchors the system during peak demand, seasonal variability, and supply disruptions. Renewables, by contrast, are driving marginal growth. They add capacity incrementally, reduce exposure to fuel imports, and lower long-term costs, but they remain dependent on grid stability and storage solutions that are still evolving.

Nuclear energy and emerging technologies such as green hydrogen function differently again. They are not immediate replacements but future hedges. Their value lies in optionality. If storage costs fall faster than expected, or if global fuel markets become more volatile, these options provide pathways that can be scaled without rebuilding the entire system from scratch.

This layered approach resembles a redundant portfolio rather than a linear transition. Each component compensates for the limitations of the others. When one source underperforms—due to weather, geopolitics, or price shocks—others absorb the strain. The system is designed to degrade gracefully rather than fail abruptly.

From a strategic perspective, diversification reduces the ability of any external actor to exert pressure. Dependence on a single fuel, technology, or supplier creates points of vulnerability that can be exploited during periods of tension. By maintaining multiple supply chains and energy pathways, India reduces the ability of any one actor to impose costs through disruption or conditionality.

Critically, diversification buys time. It allows technological learning, infrastructure adaptation, and institutional capacity to develop without forcing early lock-ins. This matters because energy debates are often framed in terms of substitution—the idea that one source must replace another within a fixed timeline. That framing assumes a level of certainty about future costs, performance, and political conditions that rarely holds over long horizons. Diversification avoids that gamble by keeping multiple pathways viable while knowledge, capabilities, and external conditions evolve.

The result is an energy system that may appear slower to converge on a single end state but is better suited to sustained growth under uncertainty. What looks like hesitation at the surface level is, in fact, a form of risk management. The objective is not to win the transition narrative, but to ensure that the system continues to function as economic demands evolve.

In this framework, energy choices are evaluated less by their symbolic alignment and more by their contribution to resilience. Diversification is not an interim compromise. It is the operating logic of a system built to endure volatility rather than assume its absence.

## 8.4 Creating Resource Security Through Political Maneuver

When physical resources cannot be produced domestically at scale, reliability must be created rather than extracted. For a large, fast-growing economy, this creation is not rhetorical. It is operational. Resource security, in this context, is assembled through contracts, buffers, and relationships that reduce exposure to sudden disruption.

India's approach reflects this logic. Instead of attempting to eliminate import dependence, it seeks to shape the conditions under which dependence operates. This involves ensuring that no single supplier, region, or political relationship becomes decisive. Energy procurement is therefore treated less as a transactional exercise and more as a continuous process of risk management.

One element of this strategy is physical buffering. Strategic reserves provide time. They do not eliminate dependence, but they slow the transmission of shocks, allowing policy responses to unfold without immediate economic stress. The value of such buffers lies not in their permanence but in the breathing room they create during moments of volatility.

A second element is contractual diversification. Long-term supply agreements are structured across multiple partners, often with differing political alignments and economic incentives. The objective is not alignment but balance. When procurement is sufficiently distributed, the cost of disruption rises for suppliers as well as for the buyer. Mutual dependence becomes a stabilizing factor rather than a vulnerability.

Political maneuver, in this sense, does not imply opportunism. It refers to the deliberate cultivation of overlapping interests that make coercion impractical. India's energy purchases are large enough, and spread widely enough, that exclusion becomes costly for exporters. Reliability is manufactured not through leverage, but through indispensability.

This logic also explains India's resistance to framing energy relationships in ideological terms. Long-term supply security depends on predictability, not affinity. By separating procurement from alignment, India preserves room to adjust partnerships as market conditions and geopolitical realities evolve.

The result is a form of autonomy that does not deny interdependence, but manages it. Resource security is achieved not by eliminating exposure, but by ensuring that exposure remains distributed, buffered, and politically tolerable.

## 8.5 The New Constraint: Critical Minerals and the Energy Transition

As India reduces its reliance on fossil fuels, a new form of dependence emerges. The energy transition does not eliminate resource constraints; it shifts them. An energy transition does not eliminate dependency; it reconfigures it. As systems move away from fossil fuels toward electrification and renewables, strategic reliance shifts from hydrocarbons to the critical minerals required to build, store, and transmit energy. Coal, oil, and gas are gradually supplemented by lithium, cobalt, nickel, rare earth elements, and other critical inputs that underpin batteries, renewable energy systems, and advanced electronics.

This transition introduces what can be described as mineral friction. Unlike hydrocarbons, which are traded through deep and liquid global markets, many critical minerals are geographically concentrated and processed through narrow supply chains. Control often resides not only in extraction, but in refining, manufacturing, and logistics. Dependence therefore becomes more opaque and potentially more rigid.

For India, the challenge is not simply access, but timing. As global demand accelerates, early movers can shape standards, lock in supply relationships, and influence pricing structures. Late entry risks exposure to closed networks and strategic bottlenecks. The objective, therefore, is not mineral independence, but early integration into emerging resource architectures.

India's response reflects this logic. Participation in multilateral frameworks, overseas joint ventures, and state-backed acquisition vehicles is designed to ensure presence before consolidation occurs. These efforts are less about ownership than about connection. Being embedded in supply chains allows adaptation as technologies evolve and demand patterns shift.

Importantly, the mineral challenge reinforces the argument against substitution logic. Replacing one dominant resource with another simply transfers vulnerability. A diversified portfolio of inputs, suppliers, and processing pathways provides resilience during periods of technological uncertainty.

The energy transition thus introduces a second layer of strategic exposure. Managing it requires the same principles applied to hydrocarbons: diversification, redundancy, and long-term optionality. The constraint has changed form, but the governing logic remains consistent.

## 8.6 Climate, Equity, and Structural Fairness

Climate considerations enter this chapter not as an abstract objective, but through the choice of energy systems themselves. In this chapter, the climate transition refers to the reconfiguration of energy systems undertaken to meet emissions constraints and climate commitments. Different energy pathways carry distinct emissions profiles, transition timelines, and structural constraints. As a result, climate commitments shape not only targets, but the technologies, materials, and dependencies that energy systems require.

India's approach to climate policy is often misunderstood when viewed primarily through the lens of moral urgency or symbolic leadership. While climate risk is real and increasingly visible, India frames the problem less as a question of virtue and more as a question of capacity, sequencing, and structural fairness—that is, whether global expectations account for differences in development stage, infrastructure, and historical constraints.

From this perspective, the climate transition is not a uniform obligation applied equally across economies. It unfolds unevenly, shaped by differences in development stage, existing infrastructure, and population needs. For countries still expanding basic energy access and industrial capacity, the central challenge is not whether to transition, but how to do so without triggering economic disruption.

This framing explains India's emphasis on differentiated timelines and pathways. Long-term targets are treated as directional commitments rather than binding schedules. The objective is to align climate action with domestic development imperatives, ensuring that emissions reduction does not come at the expense of growth, employment, or social stability.

Equity, in this context, is not framed as compensation or charity. It is framed as proportional responsibility. Countries that industrialized earlier accumulated both wealth and emissions under conditions that no longer exist. Expecting late-industrializing economies to compress that trajectory without equivalent technological or financial support shifts costs disproportionately onto them, creating new economic and social distortions rather than correcting existing ones.

India's climate diplomacy therefore focuses on enabling conditions. Technology transfer, affordable finance, and flexible mechanisms are emphasized over uniform mandates. The underlying claim is pragmatic: transitions that ignore economic reality tend to fail, while those that respect sequencing tend to endure.

This approach does not deny climate risk. It seeks to manage it without destabilizing the engine of growth that funds adaptation, innovation, and resilience. Climate strategy, from this view, is not a separate moral project. It is embedded within the broader task of sustaining development under constraint.

By focusing on systems that must keep working—energy supply, industry, and employment—rather than public signaling, India aims to make climate transition durable rather than symbolic.

## 8.7 Trade-offs, Constraints, and Policy Friction

Managing resource security through diversification and buffering carries real costs. Resilience is not free. It requires capital, coordination, and a willingness to accept inefficiencies that would be difficult to justify in a purely cost-minimization framework.

One of these costs is fiscal. Maintaining strategic reserves, building dual-use infrastructure, or securing alternative supply routes ties up resources that could otherwise be deployed for immediate consumption or investment. From a narrow accounting perspective, such expenditures may appear redundant or underutilized. From a strategic perspective, they function as insurance against disruption.

Another cost is complexity. Diversified systems are harder to manage than streamlined ones. Multiple suppliers, fuels, and technologies increase administrative burden and slow decision-making. Policy coherence must be maintained across ministries, states, and private actors, often with imperfect information and competing priorities.

There is also an external dimension of friction. Partners accustomed to stable, exclusive arrangements may view diversification as lack of commitment. In a transactional global environment, flexibility can be misread as hesitation. Managing this perception requires consistent signaling and operational reliability, especially when formal alignment is absent.

Finally, resilience introduces trade-offs in speed. Systems designed for optionality often move more slowly than those optimized for scale or cost alone. Decisions take longer, negotiations are more complex, and outcomes appear less decisive. These frictions are not accidental. They reflect an intentional preference for durability over immediacy.

Taken together, these constraints illustrate a recurring pattern. Resource strategy is shaped less by the pursuit of optimal efficiency than by the avoidance of catastrophic dependency. The aim is not to eliminate risk, but to ensure that shocks remain manageable rather than system-defining.

## 8.8 Interpreting Resource Signals

For observers, the challenge is not a lack of information but an excess of it. Energy and resource policy is often communicated through targets, pledges, and announcements that attract attention but reveal little about underlying capacity. Interpreting India's resource strategy therefore requires shifting focus from stated intent to structural preparation.

A useful signal is buffering capacity. Strategic reserves, diversified import terminals, and flexible infrastructure indicate an effort to absorb shocks through structural preparation rather than through statements or targets. These measures rarely feature in headline narratives, yet they reveal far more about how risk is being managed.

Another signal lies in redundancy. Infrastructure that connects multiple supply routes or energy sources is not accidental. A pipeline linked to more than one port, a power grid capable of handling mixed inputs, or procurement spread across unrelated suppliers reflects a preference for resilience over optimization.

Timing also matters. Early participation in emerging supply chains—such as critical minerals or alternative fuels—signals an effort to shape future constraints before they harden. Late-stage commitments, by contrast, often reflect adjustment to circumstances rather than proactively shaping them.

Equally important is what does not change. Sudden policy reversals or exclusive dependencies are rare in India's resource posture. Instead, adjustments tend to be incremental, layered onto existing systems. This continuity suggests that the primary objective is not transformation at speed, but stability over time.

Taken together, these patterns allow for clearer interpretation. Resource strategy is not best read through promises of self-sufficiency or rapid transition. It is revealed through the quiet accumulation of buffers, alternatives, and fallback options. These choices expand room for judgment under pressure, which remains the core objective across India's approach to constraint.

## Chapter Conclusion

Resource strategy reveals a central tension in India's global engagement. Growth depends on inputs that are unevenly distributed and increasingly volatile. Yet dependence, if left unmanaged, can narrow options and expose domestic priorities to external pressure. The challenge is not to escape constraint, but to ensure that constraint does not harden into confinement.

India's approach reflects this distinction. Rather than pursuing self-sufficiency as an absolute goal, it focuses on managing exposure through diversification, buffering, and early integration into emerging supply chains. Energy, minerals, and climate policy are treated as interconnected systems, not isolated sectors. Decisions are evaluated less by their symbolic alignment with global narratives than by their effect on resilience and continuity.

This logic also explains the emphasis on sequencing. Transitions are structured to avoid sudden breaks that would destabilize employment, fiscal capacity, or energy access. Climate commitments, resource partnerships, and reserve policies are designed to move in parallel with domestic capacity, not ahead of it. The aim is to keep adjustment costs manageable over time rather than compress them into moments of crisis.

For observers, the lesson is to look past declarations of intent and focus on structural signals. Buffering capacity, redundant pathways, and early participation in new resource architectures reveal more about long-term strategy than targets alone. These choices indicate a preference for durability over speed and flexibility over finality.

Resource constraints will remain a defining feature of India's trajectory. How they are managed will shape the country's economic stability and strategic freedom. In responding to these limits through plural pathways rather than singular solutions, India seeks to keep growth subject to domestic judgment even in an unsettled global system.

# Chapter 9: Sea-Based Constraints — Navigating the Maritime Commons

India's engagement with the world is shaped not only by land and resources, but by the sea. As a peninsular economy with global trade, energy flows, and digital connectivity moving overwhelmingly through maritime routes, India's prosperity depends on conditions it does not fully control. Unlike land-based infrastructure, which can be built and governed domestically, or resource dependence, which can be diversified and buffered, maritime exposure is persistent and external.

This chapter examines the sea as a space of structural constraint rather than episodic risk. Maritime stability cannot be secured once and left unattended. It requires continuous presence, shared norms, and resilient architecture. For India, the objective is not dominance of the oceans, but the preservation of an open and stable maritime environment that allows economic circulation to continue under varying geopolitical conditions.

By framing maritime strategy as an exercise in managing unresolved friction, this chapter completes the analysis of India's material constraints. It shows how sea-based vulnerabilities shape India's approach to security partnerships, information sharing, and long-term autonomy, and why the maritime domain has become central to its external posture.

## 9.1 The Maritime Reality: Dependence Without Control

India's geography confers both access and vulnerability. With a long coastline and a peninsular orientation, the country is deeply exposed to maritime conditions beyond its borders. A substantial share of trade, energy imports, and data flows transit sea lanes that pass through narrow chokepoints and contested regions. Disruption at these points—whether through conflict, piracy, or infrastructure failure—can reverberate quickly through the domestic economy.

This exposure marks a shift from earlier strategic assumptions. For much of the past, India's security and economic thinking was oriented inward, shaped by continental borders and land-based threats. As economic scale has expanded, however, the maritime dimension has become unavoidable. The sea is no longer a peripheral space separating India from the world; it is the primary conduit through which India connects to it.

For a large, integrated economy, this reality carries implications. Maritime routes cannot be secured through territorial control, nor can they be insulated from external shocks through unilateral action. Dependence on the sea introduces a form of vulnerability that must be managed continuously rather than resolved definitively.

This is the core of the peninsular constraint. India's growth depends on maritime circulation—the movement of trade, energy flows, and undersea data—yet that circulation occurs in spaces governed by shared access rather than sovereign authority. The challenge is therefore not to eliminate exposure, but to ensure that exposure does not translate into coercion or disruption.

Addressing this constraint requires a shift in mindset. Maritime security is not solely a naval function, nor is it limited to defense planning. It encompasses trade continuity, energy flows, data transmission, and the maintenance of predictable routes across regions far from India's shores.

The task is less about asserting control than about sustaining conditions under which the sea remains a reliable medium for exchange.

Understanding this logic is essential for interpreting India's maritime choices. Actions that appear incremental or dispersed often reflect the need for constant engagement in a domain where stability is provisional and cannot be assumed. The sea, unlike land, does not allow for final settlement. It demands ongoing management, cooperation, and architectural resilience.

## 9.2 Sea Lanes as Economic Infrastructure

For a peninsular economy operating at continental scale, sea lanes are not merely routes of commerce; they are foundational infrastructure. India's maritime environment functions less like a defensive perimeter and more like a distributed system that carries trade, energy, and data simultaneously. The stability of these routes determines not only export performance, but domestic price levels, industrial continuity, and digital connectivity.

Historically, maritime security was framed in military terms: control of waters, protection of ships, and deterrence of hostile fleets. In a highly interdependent global economy, this framing is incomplete. The modern sea lane is closer in function to a highway or power grid than a battlefield. Disruption—whether from conflict, piracy, accidents, or geopolitical friction—acts as a direct tax on economic activity, raising costs across supply chains with little warning.

This reality shifts the strategic question from control to continuity. India's primary interest is not exclusive command of maritime space, but the reliable functioning of shared routes over long time horizons. Oil shipments through the Strait of Hormuz, container traffic through the

Malacca Strait, and bulk commodities moving across the Indian Ocean are all critical inputs into domestic stability. Any prolonged interruption reverberates quickly through inflation, industrial output, and consumer welfare.

Sea lanes also now carry less visible, but equally critical, flows. Submarine cables transmit the overwhelming majority of global data traffic, including financial transactions, communications, and cloud services that underpin everyday economic life. These cables often follow the same maritime corridors as shipping and are exposed to many of the same risks. As a result, maritime infrastructure has become inseparable from digital infrastructure, even though the latter remains largely invisible to public debate.

Treating sea lanes as economic infrastructure alters the logic of state action. The objective is not incident response during crises, but continuous participation in maintaining predictability. This involves monitoring, coordination, information sharing, and the gradual building of redundancy so that no single disruption becomes system-wide failure. Stability, in this sense, is produced through routine presence rather than dramatic intervention.

Seen this way, India's maritime posture reflects a broader pattern observed across earlier chapters. Strategic autonomy at sea is not pursued through isolation or dominance, but through ensuring that the systems on which the economy depends remain open, resilient, and difficult for any single actor or event to disrupt. The sea is not a frontier to be claimed, but an operating environment that must be kept functional if growth and governance are to remain viable.

## 9.3 Chokepoints, Exposure, and Redundancy

Maritime chokepoints represent the most acute expression of sea-based constraint. They are narrow passages through which disproportionate volumes of trade, energy, and data must pass, creating natural points of vulnerability in an otherwise open system. For India, the Strait of Hormuz and the Strait of Malacca are not distant strategic abstractions; they are functional bottlenecks through which essential inputs flow daily.

The strategic risk posed by chokepoints lies not in their existence—global trade has always relied on them—but in the asymmetry they introduce. A localized disruption, whether caused by conflict, accident, piracy, or political coercion, can generate outsized economic consequences far beyond the immediate geography. For an economy of India's scale, even brief interruptions can transmit shocks across fuel prices, manufacturing schedules, and food supply chains.

This exposure cannot be eliminated. Geography fixes the location of chokepoints, and no amount of policy ambition can relocate them. What can be altered is the degree to which a single chokepoint becomes decisive. This is where redundancy becomes the central organizing principle of maritime strategy. Rather than attempting to control every narrow passage, India seeks to ensure that no single route, deployment, or dependency becomes a point of failure.

Operationally, this logic is visible in the emphasis on continuous maritime awareness rather than episodic reaction. Persistent monitoring, information sharing, and routine presence reduce the likelihood that disruptions go undetected or escalate unchecked. The objective is early visibility and coordinated response, not escalation or confrontation. Stability is preserved by making surprises harder to engineer.

Redundancy also operates beyond naval activity. Diversified sourcing of energy, alternative routing arrangements, and logistical flexibility across ports and shipping lines all reduce chokepoint leverage. When supply chains can be rerouted—even imperfectly—the strategic value of coercion declines. The cost of disruption rises for the actor attempting it, while the impact on the domestic economy becomes more manageable.

This approach reflects a broader pattern in India's strategic thinking. Rather than treating chokepoints as sites of contest to be dominated, they are treated as stress points to be managed. The aim is not to remove exposure entirely, but to ensure that exposure does not translate automatically into vulnerability. Redundancy, in this sense, is a form of insurance—costly, incremental, and rarely visible, but decisive when pressure mounts.

Understanding this distinction helps explain why India's maritime posture often appears understated. The absence of dramatic gestures does not signal neglect. It reflects a preference for quiet risk reduction over visible assertion. In an interconnected maritime system, resilience is built through preparation and presence, not through declarations of control.

## 9.4 The Indian Ocean as a Shared Commons

For India, the Indian Ocean is not merely a surrounding geography; it is a shared operating environment whose stability cannot be secured unilaterally. Unlike land borders, which can be fenced, monitored, or negotiated bilaterally, the ocean remains an open system by design. Its value lies precisely in its openness, and its vulnerability arises when that openness is exploited without shared responsibility.

Treating the Indian Ocean as a commons reflects a deliberate strategic choice. A commons is not ungoverned, but it is governed differently. Authority is exercised through norms, information, and coordination rather than ownership or exclusion. For India, this framing avoids two unproductive extremes: the illusion that the ocean can be controlled through dominance, and the assumption that it will remain stable without sustained stewardship.

This logic underpins India's emphasis on maritime cooperation rather than maritime alignment. Stability in the Indian Ocean depends less on who commands the largest fleet and more on whether basic functions—safe navigation, search and rescue, disaster response, and maritime awareness—are reliably performed. These are collective goods. When they fail, the costs are widely shared, regardless of political alignment.

India's approach therefore prioritizes connective infrastructure over coercive presence. Information-sharing mechanisms, joint exercises focused on humanitarian assistance, and region-wide awareness platforms are treated as foundational assets. By lowering the barriers to participation for smaller coastal and island states, India reinforces a system in which disruptions are more likely to be detected early and addressed collectively.

This shared-commons framing also reflects practical realism. No single country can monitor the full breadth of the Indian Ocean alone. The scale is simply too large, and the risks too diffuse. Building overlapping networks of observation and response distributes the burden while increasing overall resilience. Influence, in this model, flows from reliability and contribution rather than command.

Importantly, this approach does not deny competition or conflict. It acknowledges that strategic rivalry exists, but it seeks to prevent rivalry from destabilizing the basic functions on which all depend. By embedding cooperation into everyday maritime operations, India aims to make disruption more costly and less attractive, even in periods of geopolitical tension.

Understanding the Indian Ocean as a shared commons helps explain why India consistently emphasizes partnership language over control narratives. The objective is not to redraw maritime hierarchies, but to preserve the ocean's role as a stable medium for trade, energy flows, and communication. In this sense, maritime strategy becomes less about asserting primacy and more about sustaining conditions under which economic and strategic choices remain open.

## 9.5 First-Responder Logic and Stability Provision

India's maritime posture is best understood not through the lens of dominance, but through the logic of first response. A first responder does not seek control over an environment; it seeks to ensure that breakdowns are contained before they escalate. In the maritime domain, this distinction matters. Oceans cannot be governed through static boundaries. Stability depends on timely presence, situational awareness, and the capacity to act when routine systems fail.

This approach reflects an acceptance of reality rather than ambition. The Indian Ocean is prone to natural disasters, humanitarian emergencies, piracy, and accidental disruptions to shipping and communication infrastructure. These events rarely respect political alignments. When they occur, the immediate requirement is not deterrence but coordination—search and rescue, evacuation, medical assistance, and restoration of basic maritime functions.

India's emphasis on first-responder capability signals a preference for stability provision over coercive leverage.

Being able to assist quickly during cyclones, vessel accidents, or humanitarian crises builds trust without demanding alignment. It also establishes operational familiarity with partners across the region, creating habits of cooperation that persist even when political relations elsewhere are strained.

This posture also lowers the threshold for engagement. Smaller coastal and island states often lack the capacity to maintain constant maritime surveillance or rapid response forces. By positioning itself as a reliable partner in moments of need, India reduces the incentive for these states to seek exclusive security guarantees that could fragment the regional order. Stability becomes a shared outcome rather than a contested prize.

Importantly, first-responder logic does not imply passivity. It requires sustained readiness, interoperable systems, and forward-deployed assets capable of operating far from home ports. The difference lies in intent. Presence is justified by function, not symbolism. Exercises emphasize coordination, disaster relief, and information sharing as much as combat readiness.

This model also reinforces India's broader strategic preference for reducing escalation risks. Rapid assistance can prevent localized incidents from triggering wider crises. A grounded ship, a disrupted port, or a severed cable can become geopolitical flashpoints if left unattended. Treating such events as operational problems rather than strategic provocations helps preserve space for diplomacy and choice.

Seen in this light, India's maritime behavior is neither minimalist nor expansionist. It is calibrated. The goal is not to patrol every stretch of ocean, but to ensure that when disruptions occur, there is a credible, predictable response that restores normalcy. Stability, rather than supremacy, becomes the measure of success.

This first-responder orientation fits naturally with India's view of the ocean as a shared commons. It allows influence to accumulate quietly through reliability rather than assertion. Over time, such influence shapes expectations: that the Indian Ocean will remain open, navigable, and resilient—even when global conditions are volatile.

## 9.6 Capacity Limits, Trade-offs, and Constraints

Maritime strategy, like infrastructure or energy policy, is shaped as much by limits as by intent. Oceans may appear open and fluid, but the ability to operate within them is bounded by capital, industrial capacity, institutional coordination, and human skill. India's maritime posture reflects a continuous process of prioritization rather than an attempt at comprehensive coverage.

One constraint is scale. Sustained maritime presence is resource-intensive. Ships require long construction cycles, complex maintenance, trained crews, and logistical support across distant ports. Even with modernization, fleet expansion proceeds incrementally. Choices must therefore be made about where presence matters most, which missions take precedence, and which risks are accepted rather than eliminated.

A second constraint lies in industrial capacity. While India has strong naval design capabilities, production depth has lagged behind ambition. Delays in shipbuilding and repair are not merely technical issues; they affect readiness, deployment cycles, and strategic credibility. Efforts to treat shipbuilding as core infrastructure rather than a niche defense activity reflect an awareness that maritime capability rests on long-term industrial foundations, not episodic procurement.

Institutional coordination presents another trade-off. Maritime security spans multiple domains: defense, shipping, ports, fisheries, telecommunications, disaster management, and environmental protection. Fragmentation across agencies can dilute effectiveness even when assets exist. The challenge is less about adding new capabilities than about integrating existing ones so that information flows, responsibilities are clear, and response times are predictable.

There is also a deliberate restraint embedded in India's maritime choices. Not every vulnerability is addressed through forward deployment or permanent presence. Some risks are managed through partnerships, information sharing, or redundancy rather than unilateral capacity. This reflects a recognition that overextension can create fragility of its own. A posture that appears lean may, in fact, be designed to remain sustainable under prolonged stress.

Financial trade-offs are unavoidable. Investments in ports, coastal infrastructure, surveillance systems, and shipyards compete with demands elsewhere in the economy. Maritime resilience carries costs that are not always visible to the public, especially when success is measured by incidents that do not occur. The absence of disruption is rarely credited as an outcome, yet it is precisely this quiet continuity that maritime strategy seeks to preserve.

Finally, there is the constraint of uncertainty. Maritime risks evolve faster than doctrine. New vulnerabilities—undersea infrastructure, autonomous systems, environmental stress—emerge before governance frameworks fully adapt. India's response has been to avoid rigid commitments that could lock resources into outdated assumptions. Flexibility, even at the expense of speed, becomes a form of risk management.

Taken together, these constraints do not indicate weakness. They shape a maritime posture that values durability over spectacle and choice over closure. Capacity is built selectively, partnerships are leveraged pragmatically, and ambitions are calibrated against what can be sustained. In an environment where overreach often precedes reversal, restraint becomes a strategic asset rather than a limitation.

## 9.7 Interpreting Maritime Signals

Maritime strategy is often misread through visible symbols: fleet size, ship launches, or high-profile exercises. While these indicators matter, they offer only a partial view. In a domain as vast and fluid as the ocean, the most consequential signals are not dramatic displays of power, but the quieter structural choices that determine whether presence, access, and stability can be sustained over time.

A useful first distinction is between presence and resilience. A temporary naval deployment signals intent; a logistics agreement, port access arrangement, or maintenance hub signals endurance. The latter determines whether presence can be sustained under stress. When India invests in deep-draft ports, replenishment capabilities, or reciprocal access agreements, it is expanding operational reach without formal alignment or permanent basing.

A second signal lies in information architecture. Maritime awareness increasingly depends on data rather than hulls. Systems that fuse satellite tracking, coastal radar, shipping registries, and partner inputs shape how risks are detected and managed. When India shares maritime domain information with multiple partners, it is not merely cooperating tactically; it is shaping norms for transparency and collective responsibility in the commons.

Undersea resilience has emerged as a particularly high-signal area—one where intent and capability are revealed through operational choices rather than declaratory policy. Submarine cables, offshore energy assets, and seabed infrastructure rarely feature in public debate, yet they underpin both economic activity and digital connectivity. Investments in monitoring, repair capability, and redundancy indicate a shift toward protecting what is invisible but indispensable. These choices matter more for long-term autonomy than demonstrations of force alone.

Finally, consistency over time is itself a signal. Maritime strategies that persist across changes in government, leadership, or regional tension suggest institutional commitment, often reinforced by successive political leaderships, rather than episodic reaction. When similar patterns of deployment, partnership, and capacity-building recur, they reveal an underlying logic even when no formal doctrine is announced.

For the observer, the task is to look beyond momentary activity and ask a simpler question: does this action reduce dependence on any single route, partner, or assumption? If it does, it likely reflects structural maritime statecraft rather than short-term posturing.

**Chapter Conclusion**

Sea-based constraints differ from land and resource constraints in one important respect: they cannot be neutralized through internal reform alone. Oceans are shared spaces. Their stability depends on behavior, coordination, and trust across multiple actors with overlapping interests. This makes maritime strategy inherently relational.

India's approach reflects this reality. Rather than seeking exclusive control or dominance, it aims to keep the maritime commons functional. Security is pursued through presence without enclosure, partnerships without hierarchy, and capacity without overextension. The objective is not command in the classical sense, but continuity.

This logic reinforces the broader theme of the book. Strategic autonomy is not exercised by withdrawing from interdependence, but by shaping the conditions under which interdependence operates. At sea, this means ensuring that trade, data, and energy can move even when political conditions shift.

Together with land-based and resource constraints, maritime realities form the material foundation of India's external behavior. They explain why redundancy is favored over efficiency, why partnerships are preferred over blocs, and why restraint often accompanies capability-building. What appears cautious on the surface is, in fact, an effort to preserve freedom of judgment in a domain where disruption is easy and recovery is slow.

With this foundation established, the chapters that follow turn from physical constraints to institutional and social ones—examining how India works within and around global systems, manages asymmetry in its neighborhood, and translates endurance into influence without seeking dominance.

# Chapter 10: The Diaspora as Informal Bridge, Not Instrument

This chapter examines the role of India's overseas population as a feature of global engagement, while rejecting the idea that it functions as a coordinated instrument of state power. India's diaspora does not operate as a unified political bloc, nor is it mobilized through doctrine or direction. Its influence emerges indirectly, through long-term integration into host societies, professional credibility, and informal networks that connect systems rather than pressure them.

Understanding this distinction is essential. Much commentary assumes that diaspora influence is either centrally orchestrated or ideologically driven. India's experience suggests a different model—one in which autonomy, dispersion, and restraint produce more durable forms of presence. The chapter explores how this model functions, where its limits lie, and how it should be interpreted without exaggeration or suspicion.

## 10.1 From Emigration to Embedded Presence

For much of the post-independence period, overseas migration from India was framed as loss. The departure of skilled professionals was described as "brain drain," reflecting domestic constraints and limited opportunity at home. Migration was viewed primarily through its absence—those who left, the skills they took with them, and the gaps they created.

By the mid-2020s, this framing no longer captures the reality. India's overseas population is now better understood through the lens of embedded presence rather than departure. Millions of people of Indian origin are no longer
116

transient migrants or peripheral workers. They are institutionally integrated into the professional, academic, and corporate systems of their host countries. They occupy decision-making roles across technology, medicine, finance, research, and public administration.

This embeddedness changes the nature of influence. It does not operate through advocacy or coordinated messaging, but through credibility accumulated over time. When an individual of Indian origin leads a major firm, directs a research program, or shapes institutional norms, they demonstrate competence in a way that no public campaign can replicate. The effect is reputational rather than political. It normalizes Indian participation in global systems without requiring explicit representation.

The significance of this shift lies in durability. Embedded presence does not depend on visibility, mobilization, or alignment with the Indian state. It persists across political cycles in both home and host countries. Influence emerges gradually, through trust and performance, rather than through assertion. This makes it less susceptible to backlash and less vulnerable to shifts in diplomatic climate.

Seen this way, the transition from emigration to embedded presence is not a reversal of earlier trends but an evolution of them. Movement outward created networks. Over time, those networks matured into institutional footholds. The result is a form of global presence that is diffuse, difficult to direct, and therefore difficult to neutralize. It is this quality—not scale alone—that gives the diaspora its structural relevance in India's external engagement.

## 10.2 Diversity Without Direction

The Indian diaspora is often spoken of as a single entity, but in practice it is defined by internal diversity rather than collective identity. Differences of region, language, religion, class, generation, and political orientation are not marginal features; they are constitutive ones. The lived experience of an Indian-origin software architect in California, a healthcare worker in the United Kingdom, a construction laborer in the Gulf, and a second-generation professional in Canada may share ancestry, but little else.

This diversity limits the possibility of centralized coordination. There is no single agenda, leadership structure, or unifying political orientation that could credibly speak for the diaspora as a whole. Attempts to impose one would fracture the community and undermine its legitimacy within host societies. What appears, from the outside, as fragmentation is in fact the condition that allows the diaspora to remain embedded rather than isolated.

The absence of direction also acts as a form of insulation. Diasporas that function as overt political blocs are vulnerable to suspicion, surveillance, and backlash. They can be labeled as extensions of foreign states or treated as conditional participants in domestic political life. The Indian diaspora's lack of centralized mobilization reduces this risk. Individuals and organizations are free to integrate fully into local institutions without being read as representatives of external interests.

Generational differences further reinforce this decentralization. For many first-generation migrants, ties to India are personal and practical—family, property, or professional connections. For second- and third-generation individuals, identity is often more layered. Cultural affiliation may persist, but political alignment with the Indian state is neither assumed nor expected. This generational evolution makes durable coordination increasingly unlikely, and in doing so, preserves autonomy at the individual level.

Paradoxically, this lack of uniformity enhances long-term influence. Diversity allows the diaspora to adapt to multiple social, political, and professional environments simultaneously. It prevents capture by any single narrative or cause. Influence is exercised through participation rather than representation, and through competence rather than cohesion.

Understanding this internal diversity is essential for interpreting the diaspora's role accurately. What might look like absence of collective voice is better understood as a refusal to be reduced to one. In a fragmented global environment, this refusal has become a source of resilience rather than weakness.

## 10.3 Informal Influence and Structural Presence

The influence of the Indian diaspora does not operate through formal political channels or coordinated campaigns. It is exercised informally, through networks of trust, professional credibility, and shared norms that accumulate over time. This form of influence is difficult to quantify, but it shapes outcomes by lowering friction between systems rather than by pushing for specific decisions.

Here, "structural" refers to influence that arises from sustained participation within institutions and systems, rather than from deliberate political action or coordinated messaging.

One way to understand this process is through the idea of social remittances. Alongside financial flows, diaspora communities transmit practices, expectations, and institutional habits. These include approaches to professional governance, standards of accountability, and modes of collaboration. When individuals move between India and global institutions, they carry these norms with them, often unconsciously, shaping how organizations interact across borders.

Diaspora networks also function as translators. They reduce cultural and procedural misunderstandings that can otherwise derail collaboration. For global firms entering India, diaspora professionals often provide informal guidance on regulatory navigation, labor practices, and institutional culture. For Indian startups expanding abroad, they offer context on market expectations, compliance norms, and professional etiquette. These interventions are rarely formalized, but they materially reduce transaction costs.

Importantly, this influence does not depend on lobbying or political pressure. It emerges from embedded presence within professional ecosystems. A trusted colleague, mentor, or advisor can often resolve issues more effectively than a formal representative. This quiet mediation builds confidence over repeated interactions, reinforcing the perception that engagement with India is manageable rather than risky.

Because this influence is informal, it resists consolidation. No single organization or authority controls it. Networks overlap, evolve, and dissolve as careers change and institutions shift. This fluidity prevents capture and reduces the likelihood of politicization. It also means that influence accumulates slowly, through consistency rather than visibility.

Seen in this light, the diaspora's role is structural rather than instrumental. That is, it shapes environments through sustained participation rather than being used as a tool for specific political ends. It does not push policy; it shapes the environment in which policy is made. By making cross-border interaction more legible and less costly, it extends India's reach without narrowing its choices. This form of presence is not dramatic, but it is durable—precisely because it rests on integration rather than assertion.

## 10.4 The State's Deliberate Distance

The Indian state's relationship with its overseas population is defined less by direction than by restraint. This posture is not the result of neglect or capacity limits, but a considered judgment about how influence is sustained over time. Rather than seeking to organize or mobilize diaspora communities for political purposes, the state has generally chosen to limit its role to facilitation and protection, allowing influence to emerge indirectly rather than be asserted.

In practical terms, this restraint shapes the scope of state action. Official engagement with overseas Indians has focused on enabling mobility, legal status, and personal security rather than political coordination. Documentation, consular support, and crisis response form the core of this engagement. Frameworks such as the Overseas Citizen of India designation and evacuation operations during periods of conflict or instability are structured to preserve safety and continuity, not to signal loyalty or enforce alignment.

This restraint serves a strategic purpose. Overt direction would alter how diaspora communities are perceived in host societies. Individuals embedded in professional, academic, or civic institutions derive their credibility from being seen as autonomous actors, not as representatives of a foreign state. Formal mobilization risks introducing suspicion where trust currently exists, turning informal bridges into visible pressure points.

Distance also preserves choice on both sides. Diaspora individuals retain freedom to engage with India in ways that reflect their own priorities—professional collaboration, investment, cultural exchange, or none at all. At the same time, the Indian state avoids becoming accountable for the actions, statements, or political positions of a population it does not control. This separation reduces exposure to backlash when domestic debates within India spill into global discourse.

When the state does act, it does so selectively and defensively. Addressing discrimination, advocating for fair treatment under host-country law, or responding to restrictive visa regimes are framed as matters of citizen welfare rather than political leverage. The emphasis remains on enabling dignity and stability, allowing individuals to continue participating effectively within their local contexts.

Viewed this way, distance is not disengagement. It is a form of restraint that protects the very conditions under which diaspora influence remains durable. By avoiding overt orchestration, the state allows informal presence to function without distortion. In a global environment increasingly sensitive to questions of loyalty and interference, this choice has become an asset rather than a liability.

## 10.5 Economic, Knowledge, and Cultural Circulation

The most visible connection between India and its overseas population has long been financial. Remittances remain significant, but focusing on them alone obscures the broader forms of circulation that now matter more for long-term capacity. Capital, skills, professional norms, and institutional confidence increasingly move in both directions, reshaping how India participates in global systems.

Economic engagement has shifted in character. Earlier patterns emphasized household support and philanthropy. More recent flows reflect participation in risk-taking and enterprise. Diaspora professionals and entrepreneurs increasingly engage through startup investment, venture capital, and advisory roles rather than charitable giving. This change reflects normalization. India is no longer approached primarily as a beneficiary, but as a site of opportunity where expertise and capital can be deployed on commercial terms.

Knowledge circulation follows a similar pattern. Scientific and technical collaboration now relies less on permanent relocation and more on mobility and shared platforms. Programs that facilitate visiting appointments, joint research, and short-term leadership roles allow expertise to circulate without requiring permanent return. The result is not repatriation, but reinforcement—domestic institutions gain exposure to global practices while remaining locally grounded.

Cultural circulation is subtler but no less consequential. Diaspora engagement increasingly reflects confidence rather than nostalgia. Professional norms, expectations of institutional accountability, and modes of collaboration are transmitted through everyday interaction rather than formal exchange. These influences shape workplace culture, governance practices, and public discourse in ways that are incremental and difficult to attribute, but cumulative over time.

Viewed together, these forms of circulation blur the boundary between "inside" and "outside." The diaspora is neither an external resource nor a detached observer. It participates in overlapping systems that connect India to global networks of capital, knowledge, and practice. This participation does not require coordination to be effective. It depends instead on permeability—on the ease with which people, ideas, and opportunity can move without being forced into prescribed channels.

## 10.6 Limits, Risks, and Misreadings

The decentralized nature of the Indian diaspora, while a source of resilience, also introduces limits and vulnerabilities. Because the diaspora is not centrally coordinated, failures in one group do not cascade across the whole. This autonomy, however, does not insulate diaspora communities from broader political and social pressures within host countries. As global politics become more polarized, these pressures increasingly intersect with identity.

One emerging risk is the transmission of domestic political conflict into overseas spaces. Digital platforms allow debates originating in India to circulate rapidly among diaspora communities, sometimes detached from local context. This can import polarization into environments where social cohesion depends on maintaining civic neutrality. While such dynamics are not unique to the Indian diaspora, their scale amplifies the challenge.

Generational distance introduces a different form of tension. For many second- and third-generation individuals, ties to India are cultural rather than political. Expectations of alignment—whether imposed by external observers or assumed by actors within India—can create friction. At the same time, these individuals may still face discrimination or stereotyping based on perceived foreign affiliation, placing them in a position where neither full distance nor full identification is available.

There is also a persistent tendency to misread diaspora outcomes as evidence of state orchestration. High-profile success, political visibility, or collective action is sometimes interpreted as coordination rather than coincidence. Such assumptions can invite suspicion and policy responses that treat autonomous communities as extensions of foreign influence, regardless of their actual behavior.

124

These risks place practical limits on what diaspora engagement can achieve. Influence derived from integration is inherently gradual and indirect. It cannot be mobilized quickly, nor can it be reliably aligned with immediate policy objectives. Attempts to accelerate or formalize it would undermine the very conditions that allow it to function.

Recognizing these limits is essential to maintaining credibility. The diaspora's value lies not in its ability to act as a unified force, but in its capacity to remain embedded across multiple societies without being reduced to a single political identity. Preserving that capacity requires restraint—not only from the state, but from expectations projected onto it.

## 10.7 Interpreting Diaspora Signals

Public discussion of diaspora influence often focuses on moments of visibility: protests, public statements, cultural events, or the prominence of individuals in political or corporate life. While such moments attract attention, they are weak indicators of long-term influence. Visibility is episodic; structure is cumulative.

A more reliable way to interpret diaspora signals is to distinguish between episodic activism and embedded participation. Episodic activism tends to be reactive, driven by immediate events or identity-based mobilization. Its effects are often short-lived and highly context-dependent. Embedded participation, by contrast, is revealed through sustained roles within institutions: leadership positions in firms and universities, participation in professional associations, civic engagement at local levels, and long-term presence in decision-making ecosystems.

Another useful distinction is between messaging and mediation. Diaspora influence is often most effective when it operates as translation rather than persuasion—helping systems understand one another rather than pushing them toward predetermined outcomes. When individuals serve as credible intermediaries across cultures, regulations, and professional norms, they reduce friction without attracting attention.

What matters most is not how large or visible an action is at any given moment, but whether it repeats over time. When diaspora members are steadily present across different professions, institutions, and generations, it signals durability. By contrast, sudden bursts of highly visible activity often fade once the moment passes, leaving little lasting influence. For the observer, the question is not how loudly the diaspora speaks, but how routinely it participates.

Interpreted this way, diaspora influence appears less dramatic but more stable. It does not surge or recede with political cycles. It accumulates through trust, familiarity, and professional reliability. These are slow-moving assets, but they are difficult to erode once established.

## Chapter Conclusion

India's diaspora functions less as an instrument of policy than as a feature of global presence. Its influence is indirect, decentralized, and uneven, shaped by individual trajectories rather than collective strategy. This makes it resistant to coordination—but also resistant to collapse.

The strength of this model lies in restraint. By avoiding overt mobilization, the Indian state preserves the autonomy that allows diaspora communities to remain embedded and credible within host societies. Influence emerges through participation rather than projection, and through integration rather than alignment.

This form of engagement carries limits. It cannot be summoned quickly, directed precisely, or measured easily.

Yet it endures across political shifts and geopolitical strain. In a world where visibility often invites suspicion, quiet presence can be more durable than assertion.

Seen alongside the themes of earlier chapters, the diaspora reinforces a consistent pattern. India extends its reach not by narrowing choice, but by preserving it. Bridges that are informal, dispersed, and non-instrumental may be slower to build—but they are far harder to dismantle.

# Chapter 11: Cultural Logic Behind Identity and Choice

This chapter does not seek to defend or celebrate India's approach to global engagement. Its purpose is to clarify the internal logic by which choices are made, so that observed behavior is interpreted through an appropriate analytical frame.

Much of the confusion surrounding India's external actions arises not from unpredictability or inconsistency, but from a mismatch between the frameworks used to interpret them and the logic that actually governs decision-making. When expectations of fixed alignment, doctrinal clarity, or rapid resolution are applied, India's behavior can appear ambiguous or contradictory. When examined through its own cultural and historical operating assumptions, a different pattern emerges—one marked by continuity of method rather than uniformity of position.

This chapter provides the cognitive key needed to interpret that pattern. It explains how plural identity, tolerance for ambiguity, contextual judgment, and extended time horizons function not as abstractions, but as practical tools for navigating complexity. These traits are not unique to foreign policy; they are extensions of deeper habits of governance and social organization that shape how choices are made under uncertainty.

This chapter does not treat culture as destiny, nor does it imply that these patterns are unique, permanent, or universally applicable. The behaviors described here are observed tendencies within institutions operating under specific historical and material conditions. They shape how choices are processed, not what outcomes are guaranteed. Cultural logic, in this sense, functions as a constraint and an enabler—one influence among many, interacting continuously with economic pressure, political structure, and external shock.

Understanding this logic is essential for reading the preceding chapters accurately—and for avoiding analytical errors in the chapters that follow.

## 11.1 Identity Without Singularity

Many modern states are built around the assumption of a singular, bounded identity. National interest is expected to align with a clear civilizational orientation, ideological lineage, or geopolitical camp. Consistency, in this model, is expressed through exclusivity: alignment with one framework implies distance from others.

India's experience has been different. Identity has historically been layered rather than singular, contextual rather than absolute. Linguistic, religious, regional, and civilizational affiliations coexist without requiring resolution into a single dominant narrative. Belonging has rarely been an either–or proposition. It has more often been cumulative.

This internal pluralism shapes how India relates to the external world. Engagement with multiple systems does not trigger an identity crisis because identity itself is not defined by exclusivity. India can participate deeply in Western technology ecosystems, maintain energy relationships across Eurasia, and advocate for development priorities associated with the Global South without perceiving these positions as contradictory. They occupy different layers of engagement rather than competing claims on loyalty.

This is not a strategy adopted for convenience. It reflects a long-standing comfort with overlapping affiliations and situational alignment. Identity, in this context, is not a fixed banner under which all action must be subsumed. It is a flexible reference point that allows participation across domains without demanding ideological closure.

As a result, India's external posture often resists classification. Attempts to assign it a single camp, role, or orientation tend to fail because they impose a singular logic on a system accustomed to plurality. What appears externally as hedging or ambivalence is, internally, a stable condition: the ability to operate across multiple contexts without the need to reconcile them into a unified doctrine.

This layered conception of identity sets the foundation for the patterns examined in the sections that follow. It enables ambiguity without anxiety, choice without doctrine, and engagement without alignment—features that are frequently misread when viewed through frameworks that expect singular answers to complex questions.

## 11.2 Ambiguity as Capacity, Not Confusion

In many strategic cultures, ambiguity is treated as a flaw—something to be resolved quickly through declaration, doctrine, or alignment. Decisions are expected to converge toward clarity, and prolonged openness is often interpreted as indecision or lack of will. In the Indian context, ambiguity functions differently. It is not the absence of decision, but a deliberate holding of options while conditions evolve.

This distinction matters because India operates in environments where premature closure carries high cost. In a fragmented and volatile international system, early commitments can lock a country into assumptions that later prove misaligned with shifting realities. From this perspective, waiting is not passivity. It is a form of risk management.

Indian decision-making often exhibits what might be described as a "holding pattern." Positions are articulated broadly rather than narrowly. Commitments are framed in principles rather than fixed thresholds. This creates space for adjustment as external conditions change. What appears to outside observers as hesitation is frequently an effort to allow multiple pathways to remain viable until the direction of events becomes clearer.

This capacity to tolerate unfinished decisions has deep practical roots. India has historically operated across overlapping legal systems, social hierarchies, and cultural norms without requiring immediate reconciliation among them. Coexistence, rather than resolution, has often been the default mode. Over time, practices that prove workable persist, while others fade without formal rupture. The result is stability through adaptation rather than clarity through enforcement.

Applied to statecraft, this logic treats ambiguity as a buffer. It absorbs pressure from competing demands without forcing a binary choice. When external actors push for alignment, red lines, or declarative commitments, ambiguity preserves room for maneuver. It allows India to respond proportionally, adjust sequencing, and recalibrate without appearing to reverse course.

Importantly, this approach does not imply avoidance of responsibility. Decisions are made, often incrementally and across multiple domains. What is deferred is not action, but finality. Closure is delayed until it becomes unavoidable or advantageous. In a system where errors compound quickly, this patience reduces the risk of irreversible missteps.

Understanding ambiguity in this way helps explain why Indian positions are sometimes described as "non-committal" despite consistent underlying behavior. The consistency lies not in fixed outcomes, but in the method: preserving choice, resisting premature constraint, and allowing context to mature before locking in direction.

In this sense, ambiguity is not confusion. It is capacity—the ability to hold complexity without being forced into simplification.

## 11.3 Contextual Judgment Over Fixed Doctrine

Many strategic traditions rely on doctrine as a stabilizing device. Doctrines codify priorities, define thresholds, and signal intent in advance. They reduce ambiguity by mapping future responses to anticipated scenarios. This approach has advantages in environments where conditions are relatively stable and actors share similar assumptions about risk, credibility, and escalation.

India's approach places less weight on doctrine and more on contextual judgment. Rather than binding future choices to pre-declared rules, it emphasizes continuous assessment of circumstances as they unfold. Decisions are shaped by the interaction of multiple variables—timing, counterpart behavior, domestic constraints, and second-order effects—rather than by adherence to a fixed template.

A useful way to understand this difference is to contrast mapping with navigation. A map is static. It assumes known terrain and predictable routes. Navigation, by contrast, adjusts course in real time, responding to weather, currents, and unexpected obstacles. India's strategic behavior reflects a preference for navigation. It values situational awareness and flexibility over the certainty that doctrine appears to offer.

This helps explain India's discomfort with rigid red lines. Red lines are designed to simplify signaling, but they also compress decision space. Once declared, they demand response regardless of context, potentially forcing escalation even when underlying interests would be better served by restraint or adjustment. By avoiding such commitments, India preserves the ability to calibrate its responses without appearing to retreat from prior positions.

Contextual judgment also allows India to compartmentalize relationships. Cooperation and disagreement can coexist across different domains without being collapsed into a single narrative of alliance or opposition. A country can be a security partner in one arena, a commercial competitor in another, and a diplomatic counterpart in a third. These are not contradictions to be resolved, but conditions to be managed.

This approach can appear opaque to observers accustomed to doctrinal clarity. Without explicit rules, intent must be inferred from patterns rather than proclamations. Over time, however, those patterns reveal a consistent logic: avoid commitments that foreclose future options, respond proportionally rather than automatically, and adjust posture as context changes.

Contextual judgment does not eliminate structure; it replaces rigid rules with adaptive frameworks anchored in institutional practice. What it rejects is the assumption that foresight can substitute for adaptability. As conditions change faster than doctrines can be revised, India places greater trust in judgment than in pre-commitment.

Seen this way, the absence of a formal doctrine is not a gap. It is a choice—one that prioritizes responsiveness over rigidity and situational coherence over declarative certainty.

This approach is not without cost. Contextual judgment demands high institutional capacity, sustained internal coordination, and a tolerance for prolonged ambiguity. It can slow decision-making, complicate signaling, and frustrate partners who prefer predictable commitments. In moments of crisis, the absence of clear doctrine may be read externally as hesitation rather than deliberation, even when the underlying assessment is active and ongoing.

It is also not a universal template. What functions as flexibility for a large, diversified, and enduring polity may translate into vulnerability for states with narrower economic bases, sharper security constraints, or shorter strategic time horizons. India's preference for contextual judgment is shaped by its scale, demographic depth, and historical experience. Transplanted elsewhere, without those conditions, the same approach could produce drift rather than resilience.

## 11.4 Time Horizons Beyond Electoral Cycles

A further element shaping India's approach to identity and choice is its treatment of time. Many political systems operate on compressed horizons defined by election cycles, quarterly markets, or immediate alliance pressures. Decisions are optimized for visibility and near-term payoff. In contrast, India's strategic behavior reflects a longer temporal frame—one that treats short-term volatility as manageable noise rather than decisive signal.

This does not mean India is indifferent to immediate outcomes. Economic growth, political legitimacy, and security stability matter acutely. But these concerns are evaluated within a wider window. Diplomatic setbacks, delayed reforms, or stalled negotiations are not automatically interpreted as failures if the underlying trajectory remains intact. The emphasis is on direction rather than momentary position.

This long view acts as a buffer against external pressure. When demands are framed as urgent or existential, India is more likely to slow the decision process rather than accelerate it. The assumption is that time itself can be a stabilizing resource. Allowing conditions to evolve may reduce the cost of commitment or reveal alternatives that were not visible at the outset.

Institutional reform provides a clear example. India has sought changes in global governance structures—such as financial institutions and security bodies—for decades without dramatic escalation. The absence of immediate success has not produced withdrawal or rupture. Instead, the strategy has been persistence without fixation: remaining engaged while allowing demographic weight, economic scale, and institutional participation to gradually alter the negotiating landscape.

This temporal orientation also explains India's tolerance for delayed closure. Binding commitments that foreclose future adjustment are treated cautiously, especially when the long-term environment is uncertain. Waiting is not always a sign of indecision; it can be a way to avoid locking present assumptions into future constraints.

Such patience is often misread. In systems accustomed to rapid signaling, restraint may appear as passivity or lack of ambition. Yet for India, the ability to absorb short-term friction without strategic panic is a form of capacity. It reflects confidence that the state, society, and economy will remain relevant across multiple cycles of global realignment.

The consequence is a style of engagement that appears uneven in tempo. India may move quickly on issues tied to internal capacity or structural opportunity, while allowing other matters to mature slowly. What unifies these choices is not urgency, but endurance: an effort to ensure that to-day's decisions do not compromise tomorrow's range of action.

## 11.5 Managing Contradiction Without Resolution

A recurring feature of India's strategic behavior is its ability to hold apparently contradictory positions without feeling compelled to resolve them immediately. Where other systems seek coherence through alignment or hierarchy, India often relies on separation, sequencing, and absorption. This is not an absence of logic, but a different method of maintaining stability in a complex environment.

At the operational level, this appears as compartmentalization. India may sustain a tense bilateral relationship with a neighbor while cooperating with the same actor in multilateral forums. It may contest aspects of a global order while remaining deeply invested in its institutions. These positions are not reconciled through a single narrative. They are allowed to coexist, each managed within its own context.

This capacity reflects a broader historical experience of integration rather than exclusion. External ideas, practices, and influences have repeatedly entered the Indian social and political space over centuries. Rather than being rejected or fully assimilated at once, many were adapted, localized, and gradually absorbed. The process was uneven and sometimes contentious, but it reduced the pressure for immediate closure.

In strategic terms, this translates into an ability to engage without final alignment. Cooperation does not require endorsement of the entire system in which it occurs. Disagreement does not necessitate rupture. By allowing interactions to remain partial and provisional, India preserves flexibility while continuing to extract practical benefit.

This approach also reduces escalation pressure. When contradictions are treated as tolerable rather than destabilizing, there is less incentive to force premature resolution. Issues can be managed at the level they arise, without being elevated into tests of identity or credibility. The result is a form of stability built on containment rather than convergence.

For external observers, this can be disorienting. Analytical frameworks that expect consistency across domains may interpret compartmentalization as incoherence. Yet the pattern is consistent in method, if not in posture. India's actions reflect an underlying preference to keep systems open, relationships functional, and strategic commitments calibrated rather than finalized.

Managing contradiction in this way does not eliminate tension. It requires continuous calibration and institutional discipline. But it allows India to operate in overlapping systems without being trapped by their internal conflicts. In a fragmented global environment, this capacity to absorb difference without immediate resolution becomes a strategic asset rather than a liability.

## 11.6 Why Misreadings Persist

Persistent misinterpretation does not arise from ignorance or ill intent. It arises when observers apply analytical frameworks designed for declarative systems to environments governed by conditional logic. Expectations of linear signaling, doctrinal consistency, or decisive closure reflect specific institutional traditions. When these are applied to a system optimized for flexibility and reversibility, ambiguity is misread as evasion rather than as a stabilizing feature.

Misinterpretations of India's external behavior persist not because the behavior is opaque, but because it is often evaluated through mismatched analytical frameworks. Many observers approach foreign policy through models that prioritize explicit commitments, linear signaling, and doctrinal clarity. Within such frameworks, consistency is expected to appear as alignment, and intent is assumed to be legible through formal declarations.

India's approach does not reliably produce these signals. Its choices are often situational, its language restrained, and its commitments calibrated rather than absolute. When assessed through expectation-heavy lenses, this can appear as indecision, hedging, or strategic ambiguity for its own sake. In reality, the ambiguity is functional, arising from a different method of managing uncertainty rather than from an absence of intent.

A common source of misreading lies in the contrast between legal-contractual and relational-contextual modes of reasoning. In the former, credibility is established through binding commitments and enforcement mechanisms. In the latter, credibility is built through sustained engagement, pattern consistency, and the preservation of working relationships across changing conditions. India's behavior aligns more closely with the second mode, even when operating within institutions designed around the first.

Temporal mismatch compounds the problem. Analysts working with short decision cycles tend to interpret delayed closure as avoidance. Yet in India's framework, postponement may signal active evaluation rather than reluctance. Choices are not avoided; they are sequenced. Commitment is deferred until conditions stabilize, trade-offs are clearer, or alternative paths have been sufficiently explored.

Another source of confusion is the expectation of hierarchy. Many strategic models assume that states ultimately choose a primary alignment that organizes all secondary decisions. India resists this structure. It operates across overlapping systems without ranking them into a single chain of loyalty. This produces behavior that looks inconsistent when viewed from a hierarchical perspective, but coherent when viewed as a method of managing parallel obligations.

Finally, misreadings persist because restraint is often undervalued as a strategic act. When escalation is treated as evidence of resolve, the deliberate avoidance of escalation is interpreted as weakness. India's preference for keeping disputes bounded and options open runs counter to this bias. Yet over time, the consistency of this restraint forms its own signal.

This operating logic is not without cost. Comfort with ambiguity can slow response under acute pressure. Contextual judgment, when overextended, can blur signals for external partners accustomed to declarative clarity. Managing contradiction requires institutional discipline and public patience that are not always evenly available. These are not oversights, but trade-offs—accepted in exchange for flexibility, endurance, and the preservation of future choice.

Understanding these misalignments does not require agreement with India's choices. It requires recognizing that the logic governing those choices differs from the one often applied to evaluate them. Without this adjustment, interpretation will continue to mistake method for motive and process for indecision.

## 11.7 Implications for Strategic Interpretation

If India's behavior is evaluated through the logic outlined in this chapter, the task of interpretation changes. The central question is no longer whether India has chosen a side, adopted a doctrine, or issued a definitive statement. The more useful question is whether a given action expands or constrains India's future room for judgment.

This shift reframes apparent inconsistency. A decision that appears contradictory when viewed in isolation may be coherent when assessed in terms of choice preservation. Engagement with one actor alongside restraint toward another is not necessarily a signal of preference or aversion. It may reflect an effort to keep multiple pathways viable while conditions remain unsettled.

Consistency, in this framework, is not found in fixed positions but in method. Across domains—security, trade, technology, institutions—India exhibits a recurring pattern: avoidance of irreversible commitments, resistance to exclusivity, and preference for arrangements that can be adjusted as circumstances evolve. The specific content of decisions may change, but the logic governing how decisions are made remains stable.

For analysts, students, and citizens, this implies a different reading discipline. Short-term statements and summit outcomes carry less weight than accumulated behavior across time. A restrained response to provocation, continued participation in imperfect institutions, or refusal to escalate rhetoric may all reflect the same underlying objective: maintaining autonomy under uncertainty.

This interpretive approach also clarifies why India often appears unmoved by pressure to "clarify its position." In many cases, clarity itself would impose costs by narrowing future options. Silence or qualified language is not always a communication failure; it may be an intentional refusal to convert a contingent situation into a permanent stance.

Understanding India's actions through this lens does not eliminate disagreement or debate. It does, however, reduce category errors. It shifts interpretation away from binary labels and toward structural assessment: what choices were preserved, what constraints were accepted, and what commitments were deliberately deferred.

This logic is not presented as a template for replication. Strategic cultures emerge from distinct historical experiences, institutional capacities, and risk tolerances. What functions as resilience in one context may produce drift or paralysis in another. The value of this framework lies in interpretation, not emulation.

## Chapter Conclusion

This chapter has argued that India's external behavior is rooted in a distinct cultural logic—one that values plurality over singular identity, patience over immediacy, and contextual judgment over fixed doctrine. These traits are not rhetorical preferences. They are operating assumptions shaped by scale, history, and long-term orientation.

Together, they explain how India manages ambiguity without paralysis, contradiction without crisis, and engagement without enclosure. What may appear as hesitation or inconsistency often reflects a disciplined effort to avoid premature closure in a world where alignments, technologies, and power balances are in flux.

This logic does not claim moral superiority, nor does it guarantee optimal outcomes. It carries costs, demands institutional capacity, and can frustrate partners accustomed to clearer signaling. Yet it provides a stabilizing framework for operating in a fragmented international system where certainty is scarce and reversibility matters.

Seen in this light, India's approach is less about asserting identity and more about maintaining the ability to decide for itself as conditions change. It is the connective tissue that allows multi-alignment, strategic autonomy, and long time horizons to function together rather than pull apart. Understanding this internal logic does not require endorsement. It requires recognizing that India is not improvising without structure, but navigating complexity using a method that privileges endurance over declaration.

# Chapter 12: Working Within and Around Institutions

This chapter explains why India works simultaneously within existing global institutions and around them. This dual approach is often misread as ambivalence or hedging. In reality, it reflects a deliberate strategy for managing institutional risk in a world where the structures of global governance evolve more slowly than the conditions they are meant to govern.

Global institutions remain indispensable. They coordinate finance, trade norms, crisis response, and development capital at a scale no bilateral arrangement can replicate. Yet many of these institutions were designed for a different distribution of power and a different set of economic realities. Their procedures, voting weights, and priorities reflect a past moment rather than the present one.

India's response to this mismatch is neither rejection nor submission. It seeks reform from within where legitimacy and continuity matter, while building parallel arrangements where speed, capacity, or specialization are required. The objective is not to replace one system with another, but to ensure that no single institutional bottleneck can constrain long-term national choices.

Seen this way, working "within and around" institutions is not a transitional phase. It is a durable operating method suited to a plural, uneven, and periodically fractured global system. This chapter examines how that method functions, why it persists, and how it should be interpreted.

## 12.1 Institutions as Inherited Architecture

Most global institutions confronting the world today were designed in an earlier era and inherited by countries such as India rather than shaped at their inception. They emerged from the political and economic settlements of the mid-twentieth century, shaped by the distribution of power that followed the Second World War. While their mandates have expanded, their underlying structures have changed only incrementally.

Commitment, in this framework, is not expressed through exclusivity or permanent alignment. It is expressed through sustained participation, contribution of capacity, and willingness to bear institutional costs even when influence is incomplete. Withdrawal signals disengagement; parallel construction signals risk management, not abdication.

India engages these institutions with a clear-eyed understanding of this inheritance. The mismatch between contemporary economic reality and institutional design is evident. India is now among the world's largest economies, yet its formal influence within many global bodies remains limited by historical allocations of voice and authority.

From India's perspective, this does not render the institutions obsolete. It defines their character. They function as legacy systems: imperfect, often slow, and structurally misaligned with present conditions, yet still responsible for coordinating essential global processes. Financial stability mechanisms, development lending, dispute resolution, and crisis coordination continue to flow through these frameworks.

Participation, therefore, is a matter of stability maintenance rather than endorsement. Exiting such institutions would not accelerate reform; it would reduce influence over whatever transition eventually occurs. Remaining inside preserves access, visibility, and the ability to shape procedures gradually as circumstances evolve.

This approach reflects a broader assumption that institutions, like infrastructure, rarely change through rupture alone. They adapt through sustained engagement, procedural pressure, and the accumulation of precedent. India's continued presence signals neither satisfaction nor resignation. It reflects an assessment that influence over inherited systems is exercised through persistence, not confrontation.

Understanding institutions as inherited architecture clarifies why India tolerates friction within them while simultaneously preparing alternatives. The objective is not to defend existing arrangements as they are, but to remain positioned to influence what they become.

## 12.2 Reform from Within: Voice Without Veto

India's approach to institutional reform is shaped by an acceptance of constraint. In many global bodies, formal power is distributed unevenly, and veto authority is concentrated among a small set of legacy actors. India does not possess such authority, nor does it treat its absence as a temporary injustice to be corrected through confrontation.

Instead, reform is pursued through what can be described as procedural persistence. This involves sustained engagement with rules, agendas, and operating assumptions rather than episodic challenges to authority. India works to widen the scope of institutional priorities, adjust decision-making weights incrementally, and introduce new problem sets into forums that were not originally designed to address them.

This approach is visible in long-running efforts to recalibrate financial institutions so that lending capacity, voting shares, and risk frameworks better reflect contemporary economic realities. It is also evident in attempts to broaden institutional mandates—bringing issues such as climate finance, digital public infrastructure, and development-linked debt relief into settings where they were previously peripheral.

The alternative to this method would be institutional rupture: withdrawal, obstruction, or the creation of exclusive counter-systems designed to displace existing frameworks. India has consistently resisted this path. Institutional rupture carries costs that are not always visible in the short term. It erodes legitimacy, fragments coordination mechanisms, and often replaces imperfect systems with uncertainty rather than improvement.

By working within established procedures, India preserves what might be called a legitimacy buffer. Institutions that are slowly reoriented retain their coordinating function even as their priorities evolve. Reform achieved through persistence may appear slow, but it avoids the destabilizing effects that accompany sudden institutional collapse or forced realignment.

This strategy also reflects a long view of institutional change. Global bodies rarely transform in response to pressure alone. They adapt through accumulated precedent, expanded agendas, and the normalization of new expectations. India's emphasis on voice rather than veto aligns with this reality. Influence is exercised not through single decisive moments, but through repeated participation that gradually reshapes how problems are defined and addressed.

Seen in this context, India's reform strategy is neither passive nor revolutionary. It is calibrated. It accepts the limits of immediate power while investing in the conditions that make long-term change possible.

## 12.3 Parallel Arrangements as Risk Management

India's engagement with parallel institutional arrangements is best understood as a response to uncertainty rather than dissatisfaction. These mechanisms are not designed to supplant existing institutions, but to reduce exposure to their limitations. When legacy systems face procedural deadlock, capacity shortfalls, or political constraints, parallel arrangements provide additional channels through which essential functions can continue.

This logic treats institutional capacity as a form of infrastructure. Just as reliance on a single transport route or energy source creates vulnerability, dependence on a single institutional pathway introduces systemic risk. Parallel mechanisms function as insurance against such bottlenecks. They ensure that development finance, infrastructure investment, or crisis response does not stall simply because one forum becomes temporarily ineffective.

India's participation in alternative development banks and specialized funding platforms reflects this assessment. These institutions are structured to operate alongside existing frameworks, often addressing gaps where speed, scale, or flexibility is required. Their existence does not negate the value of legacy bodies; instead, it creates optionality. If one channel slows or becomes politicized, others remain available.

Crucially, this approach avoids framing parallel arrangements as ideological alternatives. They are functional tools, activated by necessity rather than symbolism. Their purpose is to preserve continuity of action under varied conditions, not to signal allegiance to a competing bloc or worldview.

By maintaining multiple institutional pathways, India reduces the likelihood that its development priorities or crisis responses become hostage to procedural paralysis elsewhere. This is not an argument against reform from within existing institutions. It is an acknowledgment that reform timelines and operational needs rarely align. Parallel arrangements bridge that gap.

## 12.4 Complementarity, Not Competition

India's institutional strategy is guided by a principle of complementarity. Parallel arrangements are not constructed as counter-systems designed to displace or delegitimize existing institutions. Instead, they are intended to coexist, reinforcing overall system capacity rather than fragmenting it.

This distinction matters. When alternative institutions are framed as replacements, they invite binary alignment pressures and accelerate institutional polarization. India has consistently resisted this dynamic. Its objective is not to force a choice between systems, but to ensure that no single institution—whether legacy or newly created—becomes indispensable.

This plural approach reduces the risk of institutional capture. If rules, financing mechanisms, or coordination platforms become concentrated within a narrow set of forums, exclusion becomes a structural threat. When access to essential functions flows through a small number of gatekeeping institutions, exclusion no longer requires an explicit decision. It emerges from the design of the system itself, leaving affected actors with limited alternatives regardless of intent. By keeping multiple systems active and interoperable, India preserves its ability to operate even as global governance landscapes shift.

Complementarity also lowers the political cost of reform. Legacy institutions are more likely to adapt when alternatives exist but are not framed as adversarial. Parallel mechanisms demonstrate feasibility and capacity without demanding immediate replacement. Over time, this can influence norms, priorities, and operational expectations across the broader institutional ecosystem.

In this sense, India's refusal to turn alternative groupings into exclusive blocs is deliberate. The goal is not to build a competing order, but to sustain a plural one. Complementarity ensures that institutional diversity enhances resilience rather than fragmentation, allowing coordination to persist across different forums and circumstances.

Parallel engagement is often mistaken for indecision when viewed through binary lenses. In institutional systems characterized by slow reform and asymmetric control, redundancy functions as insurance. The presence of alternatives does not weaken commitment; it disciplines systems by ensuring that no single platform becomes indispensable.

## 12.5 Institutional Redundancy and Strategic Autonomy

India's approach to institutions reflects the same logic that shapes its energy policy, infrastructure planning, and diplomatic posture: redundancy is resilience. In institutional terms, redundancy does not mean duplication for its own sake. It means ensuring that essential functions—financing, coordination, dispute management, and rule-setting—can continue even if one channel slows, fragments, or becomes inaccessible.

This perspective treats institutions as part of a broader operating environment rather than as fixed authorities. When multiple institutional pathways remain viable, the cost of disagreement within any single forum is reduced. Negotiation becomes less coercive, reform less destabilizing, and delay less consequential. Autonomy, in this sense, is not isolation from institutions, but freedom from dependence on any one of them.

Institutional redundancy also preserves freedom of judgment. When a country's access to capital, markets, or coordination mechanisms is tied to a single framework, policy choices become constrained by the risk of exclusion. By contrast, diversified institutional engagement allows decisions to be evaluated on their merits rather than their alignment with the preferences of a particular forum.

This logic is particularly relevant in a world where financial systems, development lending, and regulatory standards can be mobilized as instruments of pressure. Redundancy does not eliminate vulnerability, but it reduces the likelihood that pressure in one arena cascades into system-wide constraint. It transforms institutional participation from a dependency into a portfolio. Instead of relying on a single forum for access, legitimacy, or coordination, India distributes these functions across multiple institutions. Each plays a role, but none becomes indispensable. This reduces vulnerability to delay, exclusion, or shifting priorities within any one system, while preserving the ability to continue operating if conditions change.

Viewed this way, working across multiple institutional channels is not a sign of uncertainty. It is an expression of strategic autonomy applied at the level of global governance—an effort to preserve room for maneuver as conditions change.

## 12.6 Misreadings and Critiques

India's institutional behavior is often interpreted through frameworks that prioritize alignment, loyalty, or decisiveness. From that vantage point, engagement across multiple institutions can appear inconsistent or opportunistic. Labels such as "free-rider," "fence-sitter," or "selective participant" emerge from expectations that institutions function best when actors commit exclusively and visibly.

These interpretations reflect a mismatch of assumptions rather than a lack of strategy. India's approach does not optimize for symbolic alignment or rapid signaling. It prioritizes continuity, capacity, and adaptability. Contribution is measured less by rhetorical positioning and more by sustained investment of effort—hosting forums, proposing operational frameworks, and absorbing the costs of coordination.

The critique of free-riding, in particular, overlooks the nature of India's participation. India remains an active contributor to institutional processes, even when outcomes fall short of its preferences. It accepts procedural burdens, financial commitments, and reputational risks associated with long-term engagement. What it resists is the expectation that participation must imply acquiescence to static rules or inherited hierarchies.

Misreadings also arise from a preference for binary categories. Institutions are often treated as arenas where actors must either comply fully or withdraw. India's behavior disrupts this binary. It works within constraints while preparing alternatives, contributes without conceding permanence, and engages without surrendering discretion.

Understanding this distinction is essential. What may appear as hesitation or inconsistency is more accurately described as disciplined avoidance of premature closure. The objective is not to evade responsibility, but to prevent institutional arrangements from becoming inflexible constraints on future choices.

## 12.7 Interpreting Institutional Signals

Interpreting India's institutional behavior requires shifting attention away from formal positions and toward sustained patterns of investment. Voting records, public statements, or episodic disagreements often attract attention, but they are weak indicators of long-term intent. More reliable signals are found in where effort, expertise, and resources are consistently deployed.

One useful heuristic is to track where India builds capacity rather than where it registers preference. The creation of new financing instruments, the design of technical standards, the hosting of operational forums, and the placement of skilled personnel within institutional machinery all indicate where India expects institutions to matter over time. These actions involve cost and commitment, and they tend to persist across political cycles.

Another indicator is continuity. Institutional priorities that survive leadership changes, diplomatic tensions, or shifting global narratives reveal underlying strategy more clearly than alignment at a single summit. When engagement is sustained even during periods of disagreement, it suggests that participation is viewed as structural rather than contingent.

Finally, institutional signals should be read in aggregate rather than in isolation. Engagement across multiple forums, even when uneven or asynchronous, reflects a deliberate effort to avoid over-concentration. The pattern that emerges is not one of indecision, but of distributed commitment—ensuring that no single institutional outcome determines future options.

For observers, this requires patience. India's institutional strategy unfolds through accumulation rather than declaration. Its coherence is visible over time, not at any single moment.

## Chapter Conclusion

Working within and around institutions is not a transitional behavior adopted in response to temporary uncertainty. It is a stable operating method shaped by the realities of a plural global system in which authority, capacity, and legitimacy are unevenly distributed.

By remaining engaged with inherited institutions while simultaneously supporting parallel mechanisms, India reduces long-term institutional risk. It preserves access to coordination and legitimacy while ensuring that development, financing, and governance functions do not become hostage to delay or deadlock in any single forum.

This approach does not promise efficiency in the short term. It demands sustained engagement, tolerance for procedural friction, and acceptance of incremental progress. Its value lies elsewhere: in preserving continuity of action and freedom of judgment as global systems evolve.

Working within and around institutions is not a strategy of avoidance. It reflects an acceptance that global coordination now operates across overlapping, imperfect systems. Stability, under these conditions, is produced not by loyalty to a single architecture, but by maintaining the capacity to operate across several without forfeiting judgment.

# Chapter 13: What This Means for Citizens, Students, and Professionals

This chapter shifts the focus from the behavior of the state to the posture of the observer. The preceding chapters examined how India operates within a fragmented global system—how it preserves choice, manages constraints, and resists premature closure. This chapter asks a different question: how should individuals read those actions without being pulled into distortion by pace, noise, or inherited frames?

The aim is not to instruct readers what to think, nor to encourage agreement with every decision examined in this book. It is to offer a method of interpretation. In a world saturated with instantaneous commentary, clarity increasingly depends on how information is processed rather than on how much of it is consumed. This chapter provides a set of interpretive habits that allow citizens, students, and professionals to engage global developments with steadiness rather than reaction.

What follows is not guidance for advocacy or alignment. It is an attempt to restore proportion—between events and structures, between moments and trajectories, and between disagreement and misunderstanding. The goal is not certainty, but orientation: understanding where things are headed without insisting on immediate closure.

## 13.1 From Spectator to Interpreter

Global affairs today are experienced less as sustained narratives than as a stream of events. Announcements, crises, summits, and conflicts arrive in rapid succession, each demanding attention and opinion. This environment encourages spectatorship: observing developments as discrete episodes, often framed for immediacy, drama, or emotional response.

Spectatorship is not inherently careless. It is a natural response to an information system designed for speed. But it has limitations. When events are consumed primarily as moments—detached from context or continuity—the ability to distinguish signal from noise erodes. Short-term fluctuations begin to feel decisive, while long-term movement disappears from view.

This imbalance is reinforced by the contemporary media environment. Commentary is continuous, while interpretation requires pauses. Statements can be reacted to instantly; structural signals often cannot. As a result, public attention is drawn toward what can be discussed immediately rather than toward what requires time to observe. The question of "what does this mean?" is frequently crowded out by the pressure to respond.

Interpretation requires a different posture. Rather than asking what an event means on its own, the interpreter asks how it fits into a pattern. Rather than reacting to announcements, the interpreter looks for accumulation: repeated choices, sustained investments, or consistent absences. This shift does not reduce attention; it redistributes it.

A common trap in the current environment is the pressure of immediacy. The expectation that every development demands instant judgment compresses reflection. In practice, many consequential decisions unfold slowly, through technical processes, administrative follow-through, or quiet coordination. The demand for immediate opinion often precedes the availability of meaningful information.

For the interpreter, delay is not avoidance. It is a method. Waiting allows context to emerge and reduces the risk of mistaking posture for direction. Over time, this discipline restores perspective. Events regain scale. Patterns become visible. The task is not to disengage from global affairs, but to engage them with a tempo suited to their actual significance.

## 13.2 Reading Signals, Not Statements

One of the most common sources of misinterpretation in global affairs is the tendency to treat statements as outcomes. Speeches, joint communiqués, press briefings, and social media posts are often consumed as decisive acts. They are visible, quotable, and easy to react to. Yet in most cases, they are markers of intent rather than indicators of direction.

Structural signals operate differently. They are embedded in what is built, funded, standardized, or maintained over time. They do not announce themselves with urgency. Often they are legible only in retrospect, once patterns accumulate. A policy choice that alters institutional capacity, technical infrastructure, or long-term access may carry far greater significance than a forceful declaration that produces no follow-through.

This distinction matters because declarative acts are designed for immediacy, while structural acts unfold slowly. Statements satisfy the demand for instant interpretation; structures require patience. In an environment where attention is constantly pulled toward the next announcement, the quieter movement of systems is easily overlooked.

For the interpreter, the task is not to ignore statements, but to place them in proportion. The question is not whether a declaration sounds cooperative or confrontational, but whether it is accompanied by changes that endure beyond the news cycle. Over time, patterns emerge: investments repeated across administrations, technical choices that lock in future options, or silences that persist despite rhetorical pressure.

Learning to read signals rather than statements shifts interpretation away from emotional cadence and toward institutional momentum. It reduces the risk of mistaking posture for policy, or tone for trajectory. Most importantly, it restores scale. What is said today may matter less than what continues to be done quietly, consistently, and without announcement.

This mode of interpretation often requires effort of a different kind. Structural signals are rarely packaged for immediate consumption. They may be found in budget allocations, technical standards, institutional mandates, or patterns of follow-through that do not trend on their own. Interpreting them sometimes means looking beyond commentary and seeking primary material—not to accumulate more information, but to place what is visible into a broader frame.

## 13.3 Avoiding Binary Frames

A second source of misinterpretation arises from the way global issues are commonly framed. Complex choices are often presented as binary: for or against, aligned or opposed, decisive or weak. These frames simplify discussion, but they also distort reality. They force decisions into categories that rarely reflect how states actually operate in a fragmented world.

India's behavior, in particular, is frequently misread through such binaries. Cooperation with one partner is assumed to preclude disagreement with the same partner in another domain. Engagement in one forum is interpreted as rejection of another. These assumptions treat alignment as a total condition rather than a contextual one.

The analytical alternative is not indecision, but differentiation. Different domains—technology, trade, security, development—operate on different time horizons and under different constraints. Agreement in one area does not require convergence in all others. Treating these domains as separable allows for cooperation without absorption and disagreement without rupture.

Binary framing also narrows the range of acceptable interpretation. Once an issue is cast as a loyalty test, attention shifts from outcomes to signaling. The question becomes not whether a choice expands future options or stabilizes long-term interests, but whether it satisfies an immediate narrative. In this environment, nuance is often mistaken for evasion.

Avoiding binary frames does not mean refusing judgment. It means postponing judgment until the structure of a choice is visible. Over time, patterns clarify whether a position reflects continuity or drift, coherence or contradiction. The task of the interpreter is to allow this clarity to emerge rather than forcing premature resolution.

In practice, resisting binary framing restores proportionality. It allows readers to recognize that complexity is not a flaw to be corrected, but a condition to be managed. Interpretation becomes less about declaring sides and more about understanding how multiple commitments are being balanced without collapsing into a single, rigid posture.

## 13.4 Understanding Trade-offs Without Moralization

Public debates about policy often drift toward moral judgment. Choices are framed as principled or compromised, ethical or cynical, bold or timid. While moral language has a place in civic life, it is a poor tool for understanding strategic decisions that involve structural constraints and long time horizons.

Every major policy choice involves trade-offs. Resources spent in one direction are unavailable elsewhere. Safeguards that reduce vulnerability often impose short-term costs. Redundancy, resilience, and optionality—discussed in earlier chapters—are not free; they require capital, time, and administrative effort. Interpreting such decisions requires asking what risks are being managed, not whether the choice conforms to an idealized standard.

Moralization obscures this calculus. When a decision is judged primarily on symbolic alignment, attention shifts away from its functional consequences. Policies that appear cautious or incremental may reflect an effort to avoid irreversible commitments rather than a lack of conviction. Conversely, actions that look decisive in the moment may narrow future choices in ways that only become visible later.

This does not mean that all trade-offs are justified or beyond criticism. It means that criticism is more effective when it engages with costs and consequences rather than intent alone. A policy can be questioned for being too expensive, too slow, or insufficiently robust without being framed as a moral failure.

For the interpreter, the task is to separate evaluation from condemnation. Understanding why a choice was made—what constraints it responded to, what risks it prioritized—comes before deciding whether it was the right choice. This approach preserves the ability to disagree without flattening complex decisions into simplistic verdicts.

Seen this way, strategic judgment becomes less about assigning virtue and more about assessing balance. The question shifts from "Was this the right side?" to "What was protected, what was deferred, and what room for adjustment remains?" That shift does not weaken accountability; it makes it more precise.

## 13.5 What Strategic Patience Looks Like in Practice

Strategic patience is often misunderstood as hesitation or passivity. In practice, it is neither. It is an active posture that requires sustained attention, discipline, and a willingness to absorb short-term pressure without prematurely narrowing future options.

The key distinction is between drift and deliberate waiting. Drift occurs when inaction quietly narrows choices, until a situation resolves itself without anyone having consciously chosen it. Strategic patience, by contrast, involves continuous monitoring while deliberately postponing irreversible decisions. It assumes that information is incomplete, conditions are still forming, and premature closure may impose costs that outweigh the benefits of decisiveness.

This form of patience is not cost-free. It attracts criticism for lacking clarity, invites external pressure to "take a stand," and can appear unsatisfying in media environments that reward immediacy. Yet its value lies precisely in resisting those pressures. By not rushing to resolve ambiguity, decision-makers preserve room to adjust as technological, economic, or geopolitical conditions evolve.

For the reader, this means learning to recognize restraint as effort rather than absence. A period without dramatic announcements does not necessarily signal indecision. It may reflect ongoing calibration—testing pathways, building capacity, or waiting for constraints to relax.

The absence of visible movement can coexist with substantial internal preparation.

Strategic patience, then, is best understood as tempo management. It aligns the pace of decision-making with the maturity of the environment rather than the intensity of the moment. In systems designed to function under very different future conditions, choosing when not to decide can be as consequential as choosing when to act.

## 13.6 For Students and Young Professionals

For those still forming their intellectual and professional bearings, the challenge is less about choosing the "right side" and more about learning how to think across systems that do not align neatly. The global environment they are entering is not converging toward a single model of governance, economics, or values. It is fragmenting, recombining, and operating simultaneously at different speeds.

In such a setting, analytical humility becomes a practical skill. This does not mean hesitation or lack of conviction. It means recognizing the limits of any single framework and remaining alert to context. A decision or institution that appears inefficient or contradictory when viewed through one lens may reveal coherence when seen through another. The discipline lies in resisting the urge to force premature conclusions.

Equally important is the ability to move between systems without requiring them to resolve into one. The world now contains overlapping technological, financial, and regulatory architectures. Learning to operate across these—without insisting that one must ultimately replace the others—mirrors the broader strategic posture described in earlier chapters. It is less about synthesis and more about translation: the practical skill of converting standards, practices, and expectations across systems that may never fully align.

This posture also requires patience with complexity. Many of the pressures facing younger generations push toward instant interpretation and moral clarity. Yet the issues shaping the long term—demographic shifts, institutional adaptation, resource transitions—unfold slowly and unevenly. Developing the capacity to sit with incomplete information, and to revise judgments as patterns emerge, is not a weakness. It is a form of preparedness.

Finally, this approach asks for restraint in how disagreement is handled. Not every divergence signals error or bad faith. In a plural world, parallel paths are not only inevitable but necessary. Learning to distinguish between disagreement that reflects structural difference and disagreement that reflects genuine conflict is part of becoming a capable interpreter of the world one is inheriting.

Beyond interpretation, there is a practical dimension. Many students and professionals will spend careers navigating organizations—corporations, NGOs, government bodies, multilateral institutions—that themselves operate across fragmented systems. The ability to hold multiple frameworks simultaneously, to translate between different institutional logics, and to recognize when apparent contradictions are actually complementary strategies becomes a professional asset. It is literacy in a world where singular frameworks no longer dominate.

Developing this capacity requires deliberate practice. One method is to engage the same issue through multiple lenses before forming conclusions. When analyzing a policy decision, economic trend, or institutional shift, consider how it appears from different vantage points: through a short-term market lens, a long-term institutional lens, a regional security lens, and a domestic political lens. The goal is not to synthesize these views into consensus, but to understand why each generates different judgments. Over time, this exercise builds the cognitive flexibility needed to operate in environments where no single perspective captures full reality.

## A final caution

The interpretive methods described in this book are tools, not loyalties. Understanding India's logic does not require defending every Indian decision. Understanding China's infrastructure strategy does not mean endorsing its governance model. Understanding European regulatory instincts does not mean accepting their universal application.

The discipline is to maintain analytical distance—to understand frameworks without being captured by them. For young professionals especially, this distance preserves the ability to think independently across domains where pressure for intellectual conformity is often intense. In a fragmented world, the capacity to interpret without advocacy becomes increasingly valuable.

## 13.7 For Citizens and Public Discourse

In a democracy, citizens are not merely audiences to state action; they are participants in the reasoning environment that surrounds it. The quality of public discourse shapes not only electoral outcomes, but the range of options that leaders feel able to consider. When discussion collapses into slogans or moral absolutes, complexity is not clarified—it is suppressed.

One of the central challenges today is the volume and velocity of information. News cycles are continuous, commentary is instantaneous, and interpretation often arrives before facts have settled. This environment rewards speed and certainty, not good judgment. As a result, public debate tends to fixate on visible moments—summits, statements, crises—while missing slower patterns that actually determine long-term direction.

Public reasoning begins by resisting this compression. It involves asking not only what happened, but what changed as a result. Did a decision expand future options or narrow them? Did it add resilience to a system or introduce new dependencies? These questions shift attention away from emotional alignment and toward structural consequence.

Disagreement, in this framework, is not a failure of unity. It is a feature of plural societies grappling with real trade-offs. What matters is whether disagreement remains informed—whether it engages with constraints, costs, and timing rather than attributing every outcome to intention or ideology. A policy can be questioned without being reduced to betrayal; restraint can be criticized without being equated with weakness.

Over time, the most constructive contribution citizens can make is steadiness of judgment. This does not require constant vigilance or perpetual engagement. It requires periodic re-evaluation: stepping back from immediate reactions to assess whether accumulated actions form a coherent trajectory. In doing so, public discourse regains its role not as a pressure amplifier, but as a stabilizing force.

## 13.8 Misinterpretation Fatigue and Information Overload

One of the less visible pressures shaping public understanding today is exhaustion. The volume of information is not merely high; it is relentless. Crises overlap, narratives compete, and interpretation is expected immediately. Over time, this produces misinterpretation fatigue—a state in which complexity is no longer examined but bypassed.

In such an environment, the mind defaults to shortcuts. Patterns are inferred from isolated events. Intent is assumed where uncertainty exists. Familiar storylines are re-used because they are cognitively economical, not because they are accurate. The result is not ignorance, but distortion—a narrowing of interpretive capacity.

Clarity, under these conditions, requires intentional pacing. One useful discipline is delayed interpretation: allowing time to pass before forming conclusions about an event's significance. Most actions that matter strategically do not reveal their meaning within hours or days. Their effects become visible only when placed alongside subsequent choices.

Another discipline is cumulative observation. Instead of tracking every announcement, it is often more revealing to watch what is repeated, funded, maintained, or quietly expanded. Accumulated behavior carries more information than episodic activity. It shows where attention, resources, and institutional energy are actually being invested.

Finally, there is value in selective disengagement. Not every development requires interpretation. The ability to step away from constant commentary is not apathy; it is a way of preserving analytical capacity. In an age of continuous stimulus, restraint becomes a cognitive skill.

## Chapter Conclusion

This chapter has not sought to tell readers what to think about India's choices. Its purpose has been more modest—and more demanding. It has aimed to offer a way of thinking that remains functional under uncertainty.

Clarity, in this sense, is not certainty. It is orientation. It is the ability to distinguish between noise and signal, between posture and structure, between momentary reaction and long-term consequence. It allows disagreement without confusion and critique without simplification.

For citizens, students, and professionals alike, the challenge is not access to information, but judgment under conditions of excess. The methods described here—reading signals over statements, avoiding binary frames, understanding trade-offs, and practicing patience—are tools for maintaining that judgment.

In a world shaped by friction rather than resolution, the capacity to interpret steadily may be as important as the capacity to decide. This book has argued that India's external behavior reflects a disciplined method of preserving choice over time. This chapter extends that discipline to the reader: not as an obligation to agree, but as an invitation to think with care.

# Chapter 14: The Long View — Measuring Success Beyond Cycles

This chapter brings the book to a close by stepping back from individual policies, regions, and institutions to examine the deeper logic that connects them. It explains why India evaluates success over extended time horizons rather than electoral cycles, market quarters, or episodic diplomatic moments. The argument is not that outcomes are predetermined or guaranteed, but that the method by which India navigates uncertainty is shaped by an unusually long view of continuity, risk, and choice.

Earlier chapters examined how this logic appears in practice—through infrastructure design, energy strategy, institutional engagement, and diplomatic posture. This final chapter draws those strands together and clarifies the underlying rationale. It explains why endurance, restraint, and adaptability are treated not as secondary virtues, but as central strategic capacities in a fragmented and volatile global environment.

The chapter does not offer forecasts or prescriptions. Its purpose is to explain how India positions itself to remain capable of action across changing conditions, and why that orientation favors durability over immediacy, reversibility over finality, and accumulation over spectacle.

## 14.1 Time Horizons as Strategic Choice

In policy analysis, time horizon is often treated as a background condition—something shaped by culture, institutions, or circumstance rather than consciously chosen. In practice, it functions as a strategic choice. States that operate within short political or financial cycles are incentivized toward visibility, speed, and declarative certainty.

Decisions must signal clarity quickly, even when underlying conditions remain fluid. In such environments, ambiguity is often perceived as weakness, and restraint as indecision.

India's approach reflects a different calibration. Rather than optimizing for immediate legibility, it prioritizes durability and preserves the ability to adjust course over time, without treating reversal as either easy or costless. This does not eliminate short-term pressures, but it alters how they are managed. Policies are assessed not only for their immediate effect, but for how they shape the range of options available over time. Commitments that foreclose future adjustment are approached with caution, while incremental moves that compound quietly are favored.

A longer time horizon enables what might be called accumulated advantage. Small decisions—such as participation in technical standards bodies, sustained maritime presence, or the design of modular public infrastructure—may attract little attention in isolation. Over time, however, they create embedded capacity and influence that is difficult to dislodge. These gains are not dramatic, but they are persistent. They accrue through continuity rather than announcement.

This orientation also changes the meaning of progress. Advancement is not measured solely by milestones reached within a single cycle, but by whether systems remain functional under stress and adaptable across transitions. The objective is not to arrive at a final configuration, but to remain positioned to respond as conditions evolve. In that sense, the long view is less about patience as a virtue and more about time as a strategic resource—one that, when managed deliberately, reduces fragility and preserves choice.

## 14.2 Endurance Over Optimization

In volatile systems, efficiency and strength are not the same thing. Optimization seeks peak performance under assumed conditions; endurance seeks survival across changing ones. India's strategic preference has consistently leaned toward the latter. Rather than designing systems to perform exceptionally well in stable environments, it has favored structures that can absorb shocks, tolerate error, and continue functioning when assumptions fail.

This logic runs counter to modern managerial instincts, which often reward lean design, tight coupling, and near-term efficiency gains. In infrastructure, energy, and digital systems alike, India has repeatedly accepted higher upfront costs and slower returns in exchange for robustness. Redundant logistics routes, diversified energy portfolios, and modular digital platforms may appear inefficient when measured against narrow benchmarks, but they reduce the risk of systemic collapse when conditions shift abruptly.

Endurance also alters how trade-offs are evaluated. An optimized system maximizes output under known constraints; an enduring system minimizes the consequences of unknown ones. The former depends on forecast accuracy, while the latter assumes that forecasts will eventually be wrong. In this sense, resilience is not a defensive posture but a forward-looking investment in uncertainty.

This preference explains why India often resists "single-solution" fixes, even when they promise rapid gains. Whether in energy transitions, supply chains, or institutional alignment, the emphasis remains on maintaining fallback options and preserving operational continuity. The goal is not to outperform peers in ideal conditions, but to remain functional when ideal conditions disappear.

Over long horizons, this approach produces accumulated advantage. Systems designed to endure stress require fewer resets, fewer emergency interventions, and fewer irreversible corrections. They may advance unevenly, but they compound steadily. In a world where shocks are no longer exceptional but recurring, endurance becomes a strategic asset in its own right.

## 14.3 Restraint as Active Capacity

Restraint is often mistaken for hesitation or lack of resolve. In strategic terms, however, restraint is a form of capacity—the ability to absorb pressure without being forced into irreversible commitments. It requires institutional discipline, political patience, and confidence in one's long-term position. India's approach reflects this understanding, treating restraint not as passivity but as a deliberate act of control.

In a fragmented international environment, premature alignment can carry long-term costs. Commitments made under pressure tend to harden quickly, narrowing future options even as circumstances evolve. Restraint, by contrast, preserves room for adjustment. It allows a state to participate across multiple systems—economic, technological, and institutional—without allowing any single relationship to become defining or constraining.

This logic is especially visible in India's engagement with overlapping frameworks and partnerships. Rather than seeking clarity through exclusive alignment, it maintains functional participation across different groupings, adjusting emphasis as conditions change. Restraint in this context is not indecision, but an effort to prevent short-term signaling from locking in long-term dependencies.

Restraint also operates as a stabilizing force. By avoiding escalatory postures or rigid red lines, India reduces the risk of being drawn into conflicts on terms set by others. It retains the ability to respond proportionally and contextually, rather than being compelled to act in ways that satisfy external expectations but undermine internal priorities.

Crucially, restraint is sustainable only when supported by underlying capacity. It depends on economic scale, institutional depth, and social tolerance for delayed gratification. Without these foundations, restraint can collapse into drift. With them, it becomes a strategic buffer—one that protects credibility, preserves flexibility, and keeps future choices open without treating reversibility as casual or costless.

## 14.4 Adaptability Without Abandonment

Adaptability is often confused with inconsistency. In practice, it reflects the ability to change tools without changing direction. India's long-view approach distinguishes between tactics, which must evolve, and underlying principles, which remain stable. This distinction allows for adjustment without dislocation.

As global conditions shift—through technological change, market volatility, or geopolitical realignment—states are repeatedly faced with new frameworks, platforms, and partnerships. India's response has been to engage selectively, incorporating useful elements while resisting wholesale adoption. This process is neither rejection nor imitation, but assimilation: new instruments are evaluated, modified, and fitted into existing strategic logic rather than allowed to redefine it.

This approach helps explain how India can adopt external technologies, participate in new trade arrangements, or engage emerging institutions without abandoning its core emphasis on autonomy and choice preservation. Tools are treated as means rather than commitments. Engagement is structured to remain reversible, bounded, and subject to recalibration as conditions change.

Adaptability also reflects an awareness of path dependence. Early decisions can constrain future options if they harden too quickly into doctrine or identity. By maintaining flexibility at the level of implementation, India reduces the risk that tactical adjustments will be mistaken for strategic shifts. Change occurs through layering and gradual integration rather than abrupt replacement.

Importantly, adaptability does not imply neutrality or indecision. It requires active assessment, institutional learning, and the willingness to revise methods that no longer serve their purpose. What is avoided is abandonment—the discarding of long-standing principles in response to short-term pressure or external expectation. In this way, adaptability becomes a stabilizing mechanism, allowing movement without loss of orientation and evolution without surrender of control.

## 14.5 Measuring Success Without Finality

One of the recurring difficulties in interpreting India's trajectory is the expectation of completion. External observers often look for milestones that signal arrival: institutional reform secured, alignment clarified, transition finished. When these endpoints fail to appear, progress is judged as partial, hesitant, or unresolved.

This reading misunderstands the underlying method. India's long-view strategy does not treat success as a terminal condition. Instead, success is defined by continuity—the ability to remain functional, adaptive, and relevant as global cycles shift. The objective is not to "arrive" at a fixed position, but to sustain participation across changing conditions without loss of autonomy.

From this perspective, unevenness is not necessarily a weakness. Periods of consolidation, recalibration, or selective engagement often reflect deliberate pacing rather than stagnation. Progress occurs through accumulation rather than transformation: institutions strengthened incrementally, capabilities layered over time, options preserved rather than consumed.

Traditional performance metrics—speed of reform, clarity of alignment, or headline outcomes—capture only part of this picture. More meaningful indicators lie elsewhere: the durability of institutional presence, the ability to absorb shocks without rupture, and the preservation of room for maneuver under pressure. These measures are less visible, but more predictive of long-term resilience.

This approach also explains why Indian policy often resists closure. Finality locks in assumptions about the future that may not hold. By avoiding definitive endpoints, India retains the capacity to adjust course as new information emerges. Success, in this sense, is not the elimination of uncertainty, but the maintenance of agency within it.

Measured this way, progress is neither linear nor dramatic. It is cumulative and conditional. The long view values staying power over spectacle, endurance over acceleration, and adaptability over completion. What appears unfinished is often intentionally left open—an acknowledgment that in a volatile world, the ability to continue matters more than the illusion of having concluded.

A longer time horizon does not eliminate risk; it redistributes it. Persistence increases exposure to slow-moving failure modes—policy fatigue, institutional inertia, demographic pressure, and delayed miscalculation. Choices deferred today must still be carried tomorrow, often under less forgiving conditions. The long view therefore functions not as insulation from uncertainty, but as a commitment to bear its cumulative weight over extended periods.

## 14.6 The Responsibility of the Long View

Adopting a long time horizon is not without cost. While it preserves flexibility and reduces the risk of irreversible error, it also places sustained demands on institutions, public patience, and internal coherence. The long view is not simply a strategic preference; it is an ongoing responsibility.

One such cost is interpretive friction. Policies designed for durability rather than immediacy are often misunderstood—both externally and domestically. Actions that prioritize option preservation over clarity can appear evasive or insufficiently decisive. In a global environment accustomed to rapid signaling and definitive alignment, restraint is frequently mistaken for hesitation. This misreading is not incidental; it is a recurring feature of a strategy that resists compression into short cycles.

Internally, the long view requires institutional memory and continuity. Strategies that unfold over decades demand systems capable of retaining intent across leadership changes, bureaucratic turnover, and shifting political pressures. This places a premium on administrative competence and historical awareness—qualities that are difficult to sustain and easy to erode.

There is also a civic burden. A society operating on extended horizons must tolerate delayed outcomes and incomplete narratives. Benefits accrue gradually, while costs—financial, diplomatic, or political—are often immediate. Maintaining public confidence under these conditions requires trust in process rather than satisfaction with results. That trust cannot be assumed; it must be renewed continuously through credibility and performance.

Finally, the long view accepts a degree of solitude. Choosing not to resolve every ambiguity or declare every alignment means forfeiting moments of affirmation. It means absorbing criticism without immediate rebuttal and allowing outcomes to speak over time. This restraint is not passive; it is disciplined, and at times uncomfortable.

The responsibility, then, is twofold: to preserve flexibility without drifting into inertia, and to endure misinterpretation without abandoning coherence. The long view succeeds only if patience is matched by vigilance, and openness by institutional strength. Without these, extended horizons become delay rather than strategy.

## 14.7 Closing the Circle

This book has not argued that India's approach is exceptional or universally applicable. It has argued something narrower and more durable: that India's external behavior follows a consistent internal logic once its constraints, time horizons, and methods of choice preservation are understood together.

Across infrastructure, energy, maritime space, institutions, and diplomacy, the pattern is not optimization toward a fixed end state. It is positioning—the maintenance of adjustment capacity as conditions evolve, without surrendering control to rigid alignments or inherited assumptions. What appears fragmented when viewed event by event becomes coherent when viewed over time.

The long view explains why earlier chapters emphasized architecture over assertion, redundancy over efficiency, and restraint over speed. These are not isolated preferences. They are reinforcing responses to a world in which volatility is structural—embedded in shifting power distributions and accelerating technological change—and certainty is temporary.

India's method is therefore not designed to settle debates in the present moment. It is designed to remain viable as debates shift, alliances realign, and systems age. The objective is not final position, but sustained repositioning without rupture.

In such an environment, endurance becomes a form of agency—not the agency of dominance, but of continuity. The capacity to remain engaged, adaptable, and structurally independent across decades gives coherence to India's long view.

## Chapter Conclusion

The long view is not a claim about destiny or inevitability. It is a method of governing time. Rather than seeking decisive closure in each cycle, India seeks to remain positioned across cycles, operating on the assumption that today's arrangements are provisional—even when they are powerful.

This posture explains investments in redundancy, resistance to irreversible alignment, and progress that may appear uneven when judged against short-term benchmarks. These are not signs of hesitation. They reflect a priority: preserving the capacity to act under conditions that cannot yet be fully known.

Taken together, material constraints—land, resources, maritime exposure—interact with institutional strategy and cultural logic to form a coherent pattern. The objective is not dominance or final settlement, but continuity. India's strategy is built to absorb stress, adapt without rupture, and remain present as global arrangements shift.

The long view, then, is less about arrival than avoidance: avoiding dependency that cannot be exited, commitments that cannot be revised, and choices made under compression rather than judgment.

Great powers often measure strength by the speed of their ascent or the clarity of their alignment. This book has argued for a different metric: the capacity to endure without surrendering judgment. In an era where systems fracture faster than they consolidate, the ability to remain positioned—neither captive to permanence nor paralyzed by uncertainty—may prove more consequential than any single declaration of intent.

That is the central claim of this book—not that the future can be predicted, but that the capacity to navigate it can be preserved.

# Appendix A

## Three Models of Digital Governance: An Illustrative Comparison

This appendix provides a simplified comparison of three broad models of digital governance that have emerged in large, complex societies[2]. The purpose is not to rank systems or assign normative judgment, but to clarify design logics that are otherwise easy to conflate. These models are abstractions. In practice, most countries exhibit hybrids. Nevertheless, the distinctions are useful for understanding how power, control, and dependency are structured in digital systems.

The comparison focuses on two foundational functions—identity and payments—because these systems sit beneath everyday economic and administrative life. How they are designed determines who controls access, how disputes are resolved, and how easily systems can be adapted or exited.

In practice, most national systems combine elements of more than one model. The distinctions that follow are analytical rather than categorical, intended to clarify design logics rather than describe any single implementation in full.

### Model 1: Platform-Centric Digital Governance

In a platform-centric model, core digital functions are mediated primarily by large private platforms. Identity, payments, authentication, and data exchange are embedded within commercial ecosystems that offer convenience,

---

[2] As of 2026

speed, and integration. Users and merchants interact with these platforms directly, and over time, participation becomes routine.

In this model, scale precedes governance (i.e., large number of users before governance kicks in). Platforms expand rapidly by solving immediate coordination problems. Only after they reach systemic importance do regulatory frameworks emerge. Public authority is exercised indirectly, through oversight of firms rather than through control of the underlying infrastructure.

For example, digital payments operate within closed or semi-closed ecosystems. Identity is often implicit, derived from account relationships rather than issued as a public credential. This creates efficient user experiences, but also concentrates gatekeeping power. Access, pricing, data usage, and dispute resolution are shaped by platform rules that may evolve without public visibility.

The strength of this model lies in speed and innovation. The structural risk lies in dependency. Once identity and payments are deeply embedded within proprietary systems, exit becomes costly. Regulation can constrain behavior, but it rarely alters the architecture itself. Governance follows scale, rather than shaping it in advance.


## Model 2: State-Centric Digital Governance

In a state-centric model, core digital functions are centralized within government systems. Identity is issued, verified, and managed by the state. Payments and data flows are routed through administrative channels designed for uniformity and control. The system prioritizes coherence, enforceability, and direct oversight.

Here, governance precedes scale. The state defines architecture, rules, and access conditions before widespread adoption. Identity is explicit and authoritative. Payments are tightly integrated with administrative and regulatory systems.

This approach offers clarity and control. It reduces fragmentation and allows rapid enforcement of policy decisions. However, it also concentrates authority. Innovation at the edges can be constrained, and adaptation may require centralized approval. Over time, rigidity can become a liability, especially in diverse or rapidly evolving economic environments.

The structural risk is not dependency on external actors, but reduced flexibility. When systems are tightly coupled to administrative hierarchies, change can be slow, and experimentation limited.

## Model 3: Infrastructure-Centric Digital Governance

In an infrastructure-centric model, core digital functions are treated as public utilities rather than platforms or administrative instruments. Identity, payments, and data exchange are provided as neutral, interoperable layers governed by law and standards. Private and public actors build services on top of this shared foundation.

In this model, governance is embedded in design. Identity is issued as a public credential but can be verified by multiple actors. Payments operate on open rails rather than within closed ecosystems. Data flows are mediated by consent frameworks rather than permanent transfer of control.

The key distinction lies in separation. Foundational infrastructure is governed as a public good, while applications and services remain competitive. No single actor controls access to the core system. Disputes are resolved through legal and institutional mechanisms rather than platform policies.

This approach emphasizes adaptability. Because systems are modular and interoperable, components can evolve independently. Dependency risks are managed through design choices rather than after-the-fact regulation.

The trade-off is governance burden. Open systems require coordination, oversight, and sustained institutional capacity. They may evolve more slowly than proprietary platforms. However, they preserve the ability to adapt without wholesale replacement.

## What This Comparison Clarifies

These models differ less in intent than in assumptions about scale, diversity, and reversibility.

Platform-centric systems assume that governance can be layered on after networks mature. State-centric systems assume that control must precede participation. Infrastructure-centric systems assume that long-term autonomy depends on separating foundational functions from market or administrative dominance.


None of these approaches guarantees success. Each carries trade-offs. The comparison is useful not because it identifies a superior model, but because it makes visible the consequences of design choices that are otherwise obscured by technical detail or political language.

## How to Use This Lens

Readers can use this framework as a guide when encountering digital policy debates. Instead of focusing on announcements or outcomes, ask structural questions:

- Where does control sit—at the platform, the state, or the infrastructure layer?

- Can participants exit or adapt without system-wide disruption?

- Does regulation follow scale, or is governance embedded in design?

These questions help decode digital governance choices without resorting to slogans or ideology. They also illuminate why seemingly similar technologies can produce very different patterns of power and dependency over time.